THE PICTURE OF DORIAN GRAY

by the same author

LOOK BACK IN ANGER

THE ENTERTAINER

EPITAPH FOR GEORGE DILLON
(with Anthony Creighton)

THE WORLD OF PAUL SLICKEY

A SUBJECT OF SCANDAL AND CONCERN
A play for television

LUTHER

PLAYS FOR ENGLAND
The Blood of the Bambergs and *Under Plain Cover*

UNDER PLAIN COVER

INADMISSIBLE EVIDENCE

A PATRIOT FOR ME

A BOND HONOURED

TIME PRESENT and THE HOTEL IN AMSTERDAM

TOM JONES
A film script

THE RIGHT PROSPECTUS
A play for television

VERY LIKE A WHALE
A play for television

WEST OF SUEZ

HEDDA GABLER
(adapted from Henrik Ibsen)

THE GIFT OF FRIENDSHIP
A play for television

A SENSE OF DETACHMENT

A PLACE CALLING ITSELF ROME

JOHN OSBORNE

The Picture of Dorian Gray

A MORAL ENTERTAINMENT

Adapted from the novel by
OSCAR WILDE

FABER AND FABER
3 Queen Square
London

First published in 1973
by Faber and Faber Limited
3 Queen Square London WC1
Printed in Great Britain by
Latimer Trend & Company Ltd Plymouth

ISBN 0 571 10461 4 (hard bound edition)
ISBN 0 571 10462 2 (paper covers)

All applications for professional or amateur performing rights should be addressed to John Osborne Productions Ltd., 27 Curzon Street, London W1.

'I am quite incapable of understanding how any work of art can be criticized from a moral standpoint. The sphere of art and the sphere of morality are absolutely distinct and separate; and it is to the confusion between the two that we owe the appearance of Mrs Grundy, that amusing old lady who represents the only original form of humour that the middle classes of this country have been able to produce.'

OSCAR WILDE

From a letter to the Editor of the *St. James's Gazette*:
'Dorian Gray, with all its faults, is a wonderful book.'

W. B. YEATS

CAST

BASIL HALLWARD

LORD HENRY WOTTON

DORIAN GRAY

LORD FERMOR

LADY AGATHA

DUCHESS OF HARLEY

SIR THOMAS BURDON

MR. ERSKINE

SIBYL VANE/DUCHESS OF MONMOUTH

MRS. VANE, SIBYL'S MOTHER

JAMES VANE, SIBYL'S BROTHER

VICTOR, DORIAN'S FRENCH VALET

MR. HUBBARD, A FRAME-MAKER

FRANCIS, DORIAN'S VALET LATER

ALAN CAMPBELL

FIGURES OUT OF THE NIGHT

TWO POLICEMEN

INTRODUCTION

THE TORN-DOWN NEST

The Matter of Dorian Gray and the Staging of It

Why Dorian Gray? And, if so, how? One can certainly hear the questions and even some of the answers at the outset. I shall only attempt here a few answers to the questions and problems raised by dramatizing this work for the stage. First of all, I have called it simply but deliberately 'A Moral Entertainment' because that is what it is. The original is a superb entertainment; notwithstanding all the things that one knows about it and have been said so many times. It is, of course, melodramatic and steeped in the personal but painful yillery-yallery of Wilde himself. One is constantly reminded of some of the flabbiest fatboys' vainglory of the early fairy stories. Like them, it is also overlarded, full of false patches and almost sublime vulgarity, and overweaning in its grasping after an exquisitely splendid absurdity.

I remember reading it as a boy of about eleven and it went a long way towards dispelling the fatty image of those fairy stories which I had read earlier and which offended a small ulcerous reticence within me even then. I had always admired overbold gestures in the service of style in writing and in everything else and I have continued to do so. But the fairy stories were too much for my schoolboy stomach. The voice was plummy and florid, decadent but unexciting, sybaritic but ultimately tasteless and unselective. Naturally, my reaction was not as lucid as this but I think I was already aware that there are figures in art who dominate an age by the power of their creative personality rather than by the fact of what they actually create. It is obvious, but it is always the obvious that has to be restated, that Wilde the man is a much more powerful and significant creation than anything he actually wrote.

It is a proposition he would almost certainly have approved himself. For, while second- or third-rate artists often put their best work into their lives and are more interesting as people, they seldom reach a pitch of perfection which stamps itself permanently on the English consciousness as did Oscar Wilde. He was his own best creation. Good writers are mostly dull dogs. Other writers have made 'legends' part of their lives—one thinks in our own times of the Dylan Thomases, the Scott Fitzgeralds, the Brendan Behans, the Hemingways and so on. Certainly, their influence on literature itself may have been more significant and more lasting but it seems to me that Wilde opened up a free style to a general public who never even saw or heard any of his work. And in a manner itself nearer to the effect on the whole area of the Western sensibility in which the twentieth century has been inhabited—as did Marx or Freud. This may seem sweeping and no doubt it is. However, almost everything there is to be said about Wilde seems to have been said by somebody (including himself, naturally) and I dare say this is one of them. It is pursuable but not enough I suspect to do so at any length. It is a semi-proposition and one may take it or leave it.

The fact remains that *The Picture of Dorian Gray* is not only a remarkable achievement of its time, given all its faults, but the geminal story is an inspired one like, say, that of Jekyll and Hyde. The story itself is what sold out the issues of *Lippincott's* and intrigued its Victorian readers. It is a variation on the Mephistophelian bargain with the devil. But in art ideas are two a penny, as I have repeatedly told Producers, pregnant with outlines, and Writers, heavy with plot, many times.

It is the carrying through of the exercise, the form that an idea takes, which makes it take off rather than languish over a lunch-table, a bar, or the front office. Execution is all, which, as the programmers of Television Companies never seem to realize, is a very different thing from 'packaging'.

One of the things that has struck me about the original book is its feeling of wilful courage and despair, the two qualities only too clearly embodied in the spirit of Wilde himself. It is an infuriating work, often misleading, sometimes deadly serious when it should be self-mocking, and so on. For example, there was a time some years ago when the ethic of effortless physical beauty might have seemed no more than a camp, tiresomely self-abusing piece of attitudinizing.

But today? What are the things most valued, sought after? Beauty, yes; youth, most certainly. Youth has become, like death, almost a taboo subject. Everyone is not merely afraid of losing it but of even admitting that such a possibility exists. Again, youth is all important, all reaching, all powerful. It is obligatory to be trim, slim, careless. The lines of age on Dorian Gray's portrait are a very modern likeness in all this. Such a bargain with the Devil, which to Victorians seemed bizarre as well as wicked, in that they thought it thwarted nature or attempted to deny the Natural Order, is incipient in our world devoted to energizing, activating, promoting, jetting away. What prolongs active life? Why, a shot of Dorian Grays! Dorian Grays to you, man. Sin may not be the scene any longer. But *evil* is different. You can at least identify it negatively as that thing you don't like, is not to your tastes, conflicts with *your* interests. Of wrath, envy, lust, greed, avarice, pride or sloth, only pride might get a flicker of recognition on the charts. Pride has no place in a property-owning democracy any more than on a mind-blown cloud or among the freedom killers of unknowing.

So then, we enter into a world which is without a sense of sin but acutely aware of something vague but daily threatening which might even still be called evil; like the present interest in occult sciences and astrology, for instance, it is a world in which the truth of opposites is clear, if not always understood; where duality is usefully all. The only principle is that of un-uncertainty. In such a world, the Charles Mansons with their manoeuvrings, killings, bombings, hi-jackings and growing sophistication of horrors make the mild eccentricities of an Aleister Crowley seem almost spinsterish in their innocence. So far has the liberal ethos had to adjust itself to the idea of contending with, if not recognizing, such sources of evil. As I write this, one of the lame jokes around is that of the new theatrical hazard of an audience, or members of it, at least, being in danger of getting venereal disease from facial or bodily contact with actors.

The same kind of thing goes for the homosexual mobbery of 'gay' movements, with their mags and ads. Indeed the very separatism of sexuality itself has been derided as oppressive and clubbed over its limp head by the remains of Adam's Rib. Years ago, Simone de Beauvoir coined what I thought was a memorable phrase about the menstrual cycle, which she described as the monthly building up of a nest being torn down. The fragments of that nest are scattered everywhere.

All this may seem a long way from what most people will regard as a piece of *Yellow Book* melodrama. Or, indeed, whether such an enterprise as this dramatization is desirable or has any point at all. Presumably, by this time, someone will have decided one way or the other.

I distrust the method of open analogy as much as anyone but it is not difficult to find paraphrase in the world of the *Pall Mall Gazette*, Wilde, W. H. Stead, Shaw, Dilke, the Oxford Movement, the Pre-Raphaelites and Grosvenor Gallery; of self-help and opium; of laudanum and Fleet Street, of leisurely walks in gardens and dallyings in conservatories with freakouts and happenings.

It is my own belief that the part of Dorian Gray should preferably be played by a woman. As many people know, this was one of the parts cherished by Garbo. Despite, rather than because of this, this very ambiguity would help enormously to defuse the camp or period of the acting style and enable it to be played as straightforwardly, if ironically, as possible. The parallels with the historical consciousness of the last 100 years are, in fact, endless.

Having said as much, I would like to make it clear that the play should be in no way overemphatic in any of these directions. They are merely guidelines.

The set, for example, should be an all-purpose hole-in-the-ground world, reflecting only some of the aspects outside it. It is the world of Dorian Gray, clearly described and envisaged by Wilde himself and also almost pathetic in its dingy vision of the hemp trail that now leaves from the Far East and into Europe and beyond. Not a pretty sight, then or now.

JOHN OSBORNE
September 1972

Act One

SCENE I

BASIL HALLWARD'S STUDIO:
It is the world of Dorian Gray.

The set should be flexible to contain this Studio, Dorian Gray's house, and, in particular, his attic room which could be ascended by a few steps perhaps. A conservatory or small garden contained somewhere and the rest should most probably be pure dressing, *both of the type described in somewhat gloating details by Wilde and prefiguring what is to come years later. In short, jumped-up mysticism, with what Wilde calls acutely 'Its marvellous power of making common things strange to us'.*

'He saw that there was no mood of the mind that had not its counterpart in the sensuous life, and set himself to discover their true relations wondering what there was in frankincense that made one mystical, and in ambergris that stirred one's passions, and in violets that woke the memory of dead romances, and in musk that troubled the brain, and in champak that stained the imagination', and so on, and so on. In other words, tributes to all kinds of arts and decadence. Whether it be music, in the shape of yellow-shawled Tunisians plucking at the strained strings of monstrous lutes, or Negroes beating upon copper drums or slim turbanned Indians playing through pipes of brass at great hooded snakes of the period. So, a great deal of late Victorian camp objets *as well as pictures and pieces of furniture of impeccable respectability along with the rest of it.*

Jewellery was a particular passion of Dorian's, of course, and there should be room for plenty of examples of this as well as embroideries of every description, whether Sicilian brocades, stiff Spanish velvet, Georgian work with gilt coins or gold-toned Japanese with plumaged birds and, inevitably, purple and gold draped everywhere – like prose of the same style.

The picture needs little embroidery. In a corner, on a divan of Persian type, sits LORD HENRY WOTTON. *He is, as ever, smoking innumerable cigarettes. In another part of the room, stands* BASIL HALLWARD, *painting in front of an upright easel.* LORD HENRY *is the first to speak.*

LORD HENRY: There is no question, Basil—the best thing you've ever done. You will have to send it to the Grosvenor. The Academy is too large and too vulgar. Whenever I have gone there, there have been either so many people that I have not been able to see the pictures, which was dreadful, or so many pictures that I have not been able to see the people, which was worse. The Grosvenor is really the only place.

BASIL HALLWARD: I don't think I shall send it anywhere, come to think of it. No: I won't send it anywhere.

LORD HENRY: My dear fellow, why? What an odd lot you painters are! You do anything in the world to gain a reputation. Then, as soon as you get one, you seem to want to throw it away.

BASIL: I knew you would laugh at me, but it's simply that I can't exhibit it. I've put too much of myself into it.

LORD HENRY: Really, Basil, I didn't know you were that vain. And I see very little resemblance between you; with your face, and this creature. Real beauty ends where an intellectual expression begins—which is yours. Intellect itself is a mode of exaggeration. It quite destroys the harmony of any face; you become all nose or forehead or something horrid. Look at the successful men in any of the learned professions. Except of course in the Church. But then in the Church they don't think. A bishop keeps on saying at the age of eighty what he was told to say as a boy at the age of eighteen, so he is inclined to look fairly delightful. I am quite sure your mysterious young friend in your picture illustrates this. That is what is fascinating; he is some brainless, beautiful creature, who should be always here in winter when we have no flowers to look at, and always here in summer when we need something to chill our intelligence. No, don't flatter yourself Basil, you are not in the least like him.

BASIL: I know that well enough. As a matter of fact, I should be sorry to look like him. It is better not to be too different. The ugly and the stupid have the best of it in this world. They can sit at their ease and gape at the play. Your rank and wealth, Henry; my art—whatever that might be worth or not; Dorian Gray's looks—oh, we'll all suffer for what the Gods have loaded us with.

LORD HENRY: Dorian Gray? So that's his name?

BASIL: Yes. I didn't mean to tell you.

LORD HENRY: But why not?

BASIL: People I like—I don't give their names. It is like giving them up. I've come to love secrecy. It seems to be the one thing that can begin to make life mysterious or even better. I never tell people where I have gone to. I suppose you think it's a bit potty?

LORD HENRY: Not at all, my dear Basil. You seem to forget that I am married and the one charm of marriage is that it makes a life of deception absolutely necessary for both parties. I never know where my wife is, and my wife never knows what I am doing. We tell each other the most absurd stories with the most serious faces. My wife is very good at it— much better, in fact, than I am.

BASIL: It's my belief that you really are a very good husband, but that you are thoroughly ashamed of your own virtues. As you would say, you never say a moral thing and you never do a wrong thing. Your cynicism is simply a pose.

LORD HENRY: Being natural is simply a pose and the most irritating pose I know. Basil, I want you to explain to me why you won't exhibit Dorian Gray's picture. I want the *real* reason.

BASIL: I told you the real reason.

LORD HENRY: No, you said it was because there was too much of yourself in it, which is childish.

BASIL: Harry, I think every portrait that is painted with feeling is a portrait of the artist rather than the sitter. He is merely the accident, the occasion . . .

LORD HENRY: I can believe anything provided it is quite incredible . . .

BASIL: Two months ago I simply went to a crush at Lady
Brandon's—you know how we artists have to show ourselves
in Society from time to time, just to remind the public
that we exist at all—well, after I had been in the room
about ten minutes, I suddenly became conscious of
someone looking at me. I turned around and saw Dorian
Gray for the first time. Our eyes met and I can only tell you
that a curious sensation of terror came over me and something seemed to tell me that I was on the verge of some
crisis in my life. I turned away to get out of the room. It
wasn't conscience but cowardice of some kind.

LORD HENRY: Conscience and cowardice are really the same
things; Basil, conscience is the trade name of the firm, that's
all.

BASIL: I don't believe that, Harry, and I don't believe you do
either. However, whatever my motive was—perhaps it was
pride—I certainly tried to get my way out of the door. Then,
of course, I was waylaid by Lady Brandon—'Not going away
so soon, Mr. Hallward?' she screamed it out at me in that
way of hers.

LORD HENRY: Yes, she's a peacock in everything except beauty.

BASIL: Anyway, I couldn't get rid of her. Suddenly I found
myself face to face with this young man and his—
personality. We were quite close by this time and I asked
Lady Brandon to introduce me.

LORD HENRY: And how did she describe this extraordinary fellow?
She usually treats her guests exactly like an auctioneer treats
his goods. She either explains them entirely away, or tells
one everything about them except what one wants to know.

BASIL: You are rather hard on her, Harry.

LORD HENRY: My dear friend, she tried to found a salon and only
succeeded in opening a restaurant. How could one admire
her? But, tell me, what did she eventually say?

BASIL: Oh, something like 'quite forget what he does—afraid he
—doesn't do anything—oh, yes, plays the piano—or is it the
violin, Mr. Gray?' Neither of us could help laughing at that
one and we seemed to become friends right away.

LORD HENRY: Laughter isn't at all a bad beginning for a friendship and it's far the best ending for one.

BASIL: You don't understand what friendship is, Harry. Or what enmity is, for that matter. You like everyone; that's to say, you are indifferent to everyone.

LORD HENRY: I choose my friends for their good looks, my acquaintances for their good characters, and my enemies for their good intellects. A man can't be too careful in the choice of his enemies. I haven't got one who is a fool. They are all men of some intellectual power, and consequently they all appreciate me.

BASIL: According to your category I must be merely an acquaintance, a sort of brother.

LORD HENRY: Oh, brothers! I don't care for brothers. My elder brother won't die and my younger brothers never seem to do anything else. If one puts forward an idea to a true Englishman—always a rash thing to do—he never dreams of considering whether it is right or wrong. Only whether one believes it oneself. But I like persons better than principles. Tell me more about Dorian Gray.

BASIL: He is absolutely necessary to my art—at the moment—almost daily. I sometimes think there are only two eras of artistic importance. The first is the appearance of a new medium and the other is the appearance of a new personality to express it. And he is much more than a model or a sitter. I tell you, what I have done of him is the best work of my life. We've all invented a realism that is vulgar or an ideality that's void. Dorian Gray is a new harmony. It's *there*, and I've always missed it.

LORD HENRY: Basil, this is extraordinary! I must see him . . .

BASIL: He's simply a motive to me. You might see nothing in him. I think I shall see everything. That's all.

LORD HENRY: Then why won't you exhibit the portrait?

BASIL: Because there might seem to certain shallow, prying eyes, a curious artistic idolatry. We live in an age when people think of art as a form of autobiography. I don't want that for him or myself.

LORD HENRY: Is he fond of you?

BASIL: He likes me I think . . . Although, now and then, he seems to take a real delight in giving me pain. I flatter him.

LORD HENRY: Perhaps you will tire sooner than he will. Genius lasts longer than beauty. Which is why we take such pains to overeducate ourselves. The thoroughly well-informed man —that is the modern ideal. Like a bric-a-brac shop, with everything priced above its proper value. What you have told me is a romance of art, and like any kind of romance, it leaves one so unromantic.

BASIL: Not me, Harry. You can't feel what I feel; you change too often.

LORD HENRY: Those who are always faithful know only the trivial side of love. It's the faithless who know the tragedies . . . I've just remembered . . .

BASIL: What?

LORD HENRY: The name. My aunt, Lady Agatha, told me she'd discovered a wonderful young creature who's going to help her in the East End. She never said anything about being good-looking.

BASIL: I don't want you to meet him.

LORD HENRY: I think I see him coming already. You'll *have* to introduce me now.

BASIL: Dorian Gray has a simple and beautiful nature. Don't try to *influence*. For my sake, and my work's sake. Mind, Harry, I'm trusting you.

LORD HENRY: What nonsense you do talk! Come!
(*Enter* DORIAN GRAY.)

DORIAN: I beg your pardon, Basil. I didn't know you had anyone with you.

BASIL: This is Lord Henry Wotton, Dorian. An old Oxford friend.

LORD HENRY: He's just been telling me what a fine sitter you are. You are also one of my aunt's favourite victims, I'm afraid.

DORIAN: I am in Lady Agatha's black books at present. I promised to go to a club in Whitechapel with her last Tuesday. Do you know—I really forgot all about it?

LORD HENRY: You look genuinely contrite about it. Oh, I will make your peace with my aunt. She's quite devoted to you. And I don't think it really matters about your not being there. You are far too serious to go in for philanthropy, Mr. Gray. And *profound*.

(LORD HENRY *flings himself down on the divan and opens his cigarette case while* BASIL *prepares his colours and brushes.*)

BASIL: Harry, I do want to get this finished today. Do go off to one of your things or something . . .

LORD HENRY (*at* DORIAN): It seems I'm unwanted.

DORIAN: Don't go. Basil is only in one of his starting-order sulks. And I'd like to know why you think I shouldn't 'go in' for philanthropy.

LORD HENRY: You don't really mind, Basil, do you? You've often told me you like your sitters to have someone to chat to.

BASIL: There's not much left to do. And Dorian's whims are laws to everyone, except himself. So just stay and sit down again, Harry, and you, Dorian, get up on the platform and don't move about too much. Or pay any attention to what *he* says. He's a bad influence over all his friends except me . . .

(DORIAN *steps up on to the dais.*)

DORIAN: Is your influence really as bad as that?

LORD HENRY: There is no such thing as a good influence, which is simply a way of saying that you hand him your soul. The one who takes that over is unnatural. Like his thoughts or passions, his virtues are not real to him. His sins are borrowed ones, the actor of a part that's not written for him. To realize one's *own* nature as perfectly as one can— that's what we're for. People have forgotten the highest of all duties. The duty that one owes to oneself. Of course, they are charitable. But their own souls starve and go naked. Courage has gone out of our race. Perhaps we never really had it.

BASIL: Dorian, head a little more to the right, that's a good boy . . .

LORD HENRY: Yet, somehow I still believe that if a man were to live out his life fully and completely . . .

DORIAN: Yes?

LORD HENRY: Give form to every thought, expression to every idea and so on, well, the world might forget its past maladies. We're punished for our refusals. The body sins once, and has done with it. Action is a mode of purification. Nothing left but the remembrance of pleasure. Or the luxury of regret. It's in the brain, and the brain alone, that the great sins of the world take place. *You* must know that, Mr. Gray; had passions that made you afraid, thoughts that filled you with terror . . . day dreams and sleeping dreams——

DORIAN: Please stop . . . There's some answer to all you're saying. I know but I can't find it for the moment. I'd like to think. Or *not* to . . .

(*There is silence as* DORIAN *stands,* BASIL *works away at his canvas and* LORD HENRY *looks on. Then:*)

Basil, I'm getting weary standing up here.

BASIL: Just a few more——

DORIAN: It seems stifling in here today. I must have some air.

BASIL: I'm so sorry. When I'm working, I tend to forget these things. It was better than ever then. Stillness . . . I don't know what Harry's been on about, but you certainly——

DORIAN: Weren't being paid compliments if that's——

BASIL: Whatever it was, don't believe a word he says.

LORD HENRY: Why shouldn't he believe me? It *is* terribly hot in the studio, Basil. Let's have something iced to drink, something with strawberries in.

BASIL (*working on absently*): I'll see to it. I've got to work up this background. But don't keep him too long. I've not been in form like this. This is going to be . . . it . . . as it is.

(*The other two men move over to the small, flowered area leaving* BASIL *behind his easel.*)

LORD HENRY: He's right. You are indeed a wonderful creation. You know more than you think you know. Just as you know less than you want to know.

(DORIAN *is disturbed.*)

You mustn't let yourself become sunburnt. It would be most unbecoming.

DORIAN (*laughs*): What could it possibly matter?

LORD HENRY: It should matter everything to you.

DORIAN: Why?

LORD HENRY: You have the most marvellous *youth*. And that is the one thing worth having.

DORIAN: Well, I don't feel that, Lord Henry.

LORD HENRY: Don't frown so, Mr. Gray. Beauty is a form of genius. Higher, in fact. It requires no explaining. It is one of the great facts of the world. Like sunlight on water or the darkness of seasons. Or whatever we call these things. It makes princes of those who have it. You smile? Ah—when you have lost it will be no time to smile . . . You may think that beauty—but, to me, nothing is more superficial than *thought*. It's only shallow people who don't judge by appearances. The mystery of the world is in the visible. Not the invisible. Yes, Mr. Gray. The Gods have been good to you. For the present. But don't, don't, squander the gold of your days. Listening to the tedious, trying to improve the hopeless failure of it, the false ideals of our age. Let nothing be lost upon you. Be afraid of nothing. A new *sensation*—horizon— that is what our century wants. You might be its visible— oh, symbol, if you like. The reaches of your personality are endless. For a season.

(*Pause.*)

The moment I met you I saw that you were unconscious of what you might be. I felt I must tell you. The twenty-year pulse becomes sluggish. Limbs fail. Senses rot. Become cringing puppetry . . . Youth—no . . . there is absolutely nothing else in the world.

(*Pause.* BASIL *comes over to them.*)

BASIL: Dorian—I *am* waiting!

(*They follow him.*)

LORD HENRY: You *are* glad you have met me, Mr. Gray?

DORIAN: Glad now. I wonder if I shall always be?

LORD HENRY: Always! What a dreadful word it is. Women are so fond of using it. They spoil every romance by trying to make it last forever. It's also a meaningless word. The only difference between a caprice and a lifelong passion is that the caprice lasts slightly longer.

DORIAN: In that case, perhaps our friendship should be a caprice.

BASIL: It's done. No more, as I'd *thought*. It's quite done. Just now . . .

(LORD HENRY *goes over and examines the picture, which is not visible to the audience.*)

LORD HENRY: My dear fellow, you must be over the moon. It's the most fantastic modern portrait I've ever seen. It really is. Mr. Gray, come over and look at yourself.

DORIAN: Is it really finished?

BASIL: Quite finished. I thought we'd do nothing today. It's as if it did itself. I can't say how grateful I am——

LORD HENRY: That's entirely due to me. Isn't it?

(DORIAN *does not reply but passes over to look at his picture. When he does so, it is clear that he is more than pleased. As if he recognizes his likeness for the first time. He stands in front of it, motionless with curiosity and wonder. Then he backs away slightly, almost as if he had been struck.*)

BASIL: Dorian! What is it? Don't you like it?

LORD HENRY: Of course he likes it. Who wouldn't? I will give you anything you like to ask for it. I must have it.

BASIL: It's not my property, Harry.

LORD HENRY: Whose property is it?

BASIL: Dorian's, of course.

LORD HENRY: He's a very lucky fellow.

DORIAN: This picture will always remain young. It will never be older than, than this particular day in June . . . If only it were the other way around. One would give anything for that.

LORD HENRY: You'd hardly care for such an arrangement, Basil. Rather hard lines on your work.

BASIL: I'd object very strongly.

DORIAN: I'm sure you would, Basil. (*Turning on him.*) You like your art better than your friends. I'm no more to you than one of your green bronze figures is. Not as much, I should think.

(BASIL *is astonished by this sudden attack.*)

BASIL: Dorian, don't say things like that.

DORIAN: Your picture has taught me. Lord Henry Wotton is perfectly right. When I do find I'm growing old I shall simply kill myself . . .

BASIL: I have never had such a friend as you. You tell me that you are jealous, or could be, of, well, material things, in such a way? *You* are finer than *any* of them.

DORIAN: I'm jealous of that portrait. Why should it keep what I lose? Every moment it takes something from *me*. If only it could all change. Why did you paint it! So that one day I shall be mocked by it!

(*Pause.*)

BASIL: This is your doing, Harry.

LORD HENRY: It is the real Dorian Gray. That is all.

BASIL: It is not.

LORD HENRY: If it is not, what have I got to do with it?

BASIL: Harry, I can't quarrel with my two best friends at once but, between you, you have made me hate the finest piece of work I have ever done. Very well. I'll destroy it. It's only colour and canvas. I won't let it cut across three lives and—apparently mar them.

(*He goes to the deal painting-table, takes up a long palette knife, and, turning to rip at the picture quite systematically, is stopped by* DORIAN. *The knife is grabbed from him and torn out of his hand, and thrown across the room.*)

DORIAN: Don't, Basil! Don't! It would be a murder.

BASIL (*coldly*): I'm glad you appreciate my work at last. I never thought you would.

DORIAN: Appreciate it? It's part of myself. I feel it . . .

BASIL: Well, as soon as you are dry, you shall be varnished, and framed, and sent home. You'll have some tea, Dorian? And you, Harry? Or do you object to simple pleasures?

LORD HENRY: I adore simple pleasures. They are the last refuge of the complex. But I don't like scenes, except on the stage. Man may be many things but he is not rational. And glad I am he's not, after all. I just wish you two wouldn't squabble over this picture. You'd much better let me have it, Basil. This silly boy doesn't really want it. And I really do.

DORIAN: If you let anyone but me have it—I shall never forgive you. (*To* LORD HENRY.) And nobody calls me silly boy!

BASIL: The picture's yours, Dorian. You know that . . . I gave it to you before it existed.

LORD HENRY: Also, you know quite well that you have been a little silly. And you don't really object to reminders of looking young.

DORIAN: I'd have objected very strongly this morning.

LORD HENRY: Ah, this morning! You have lived since then . . .
Let's go to the theatre tonight. There's sure to be something on, somewhere. I had promised to dine at White's but
it was only with an old friend, so I can send a wire saying
I'm prevented from coming because of a subsequent
engagement. That would be rather a nice excuse. Yes, it
will have all the surprise of candour.

BASIL: It's such a bore putting on dress-clothes.

LORD HENRY: Yes, the costume of the nineteenth century is
awful. Sin is the only real colour-element left in modern
life.

DORIAN: I'd like to come with you, if I may.

LORD HENRY: Then you shall. And you too, Basil. Won't you?

BASIL: I can't really. I'd sooner not. I've a lot of work to do.

LORD HENRY: Well then, you and I shall go alone, Mr. Gray.

BASIL: I shall stay with the real Dorian.

DORIAN: Is it the real Dorian? Am I really like that?

BASIL: Yes. You are just like that.

DORIAN: I'd hope to . . .

BASIL: At least, you are like it in appearance, but *it* will never
alter. That's something.

LORD HENRY: Young men want to be faithful and aren't. Old men
want to be faithless and can't.

BASIL: Don't go to the theatre tonight, Dorian. Stay and dine
with me.

DORIAN: I can't.

BASIL: Why?

DORIAN: Because I've promised to go to the theatre.

BASIL: He won't like you any better for keeping promises. Don't
go. (DORIAN *stands unmoved.*)
Please.
(DORIAN *hesitates. Then sees* LORD HENRY's *amused smile.*)

DORIAN: I'm going, Basil.

BASIL: Very well. And now, it's rather late and, as you have to
dress, you'd better lose no more time. Good-bye, Harry.
Good-bye, Dorian. Come and see me soon. Come

tomorrow.

DORIAN: Certainly.

BASIL: You won't forget?

DORIAN: No, of course not.

BASIL (*to* LORD HENRY): Remember——

LORD HENRY: I remember. Come, Mr. Gray. My hansom is outside. I can drop you off at your place. Good-bye, Basil. It's been a most interesting afternoon . . .

(*They go off, leaving* BASIL *alone. He sinks down on to his sofa, a look of pain crossing his face.*)

FADE

SCENE II

Seated in an armchair is LORD HENRY'*s uncle,* LORD FERMOR. *He puts down the copy of* The Times *he is reading as his nephew enters.*

LORD FERMOR: What's got you out so early? I thought you dandies never got up till two and weren't visible till five.

LORD HENRY: Pure family affection, I assure you, Uncle George. I want to get something out of you.

LORD FERMOR: Money, I suppose. Young people nowadays imagine that money's everything.

LORD HENRY: Yes, and when they grow older, they know it. But it isn't money I want. It's only people who pay their bills who want that, Uncle George. And I never pay mine. Credit is the capital of a younger son. And one lives quite adequately on it. Besides, I always deal with brother Dartmoor's tradesmen, and consequently they never bother me at all. What I want is information. Useless information, naturally.

LORD FERMOR: I can tell you anything that's in an English Blue-book. Though nowadays these fellows write such a lot of nonsense. When I was in the Diplomatic, things were much better. But now I hear they let them in by examination. What can you expect? Examinations, sir, are pure humbug from beginning to end. If a man is a gentleman he knows

29

quite enough, and if he isn't a gentleman, whatever he knows is bad for him.

LORD HENRY: Mr. Dorian Gray does not belong to Blue-books, Uncle George.

LORD FERMOR: Mr. Dorian Gray ? Who is he?

LORD HENRY: That is what I've come to learn, Uncle George. Or rather, I know who he is. He's the last Lord Kelso's grandson and his mother was a Devereux; Lady Margaret Devereux. I want you to tell men about *her*. Whom did she marry, for instance. You've know nearly everyone in your time.

LORD FERMOR: Of course I knew her. Extraordinarily beautiful girl. Made all the men frantic running away with a penniless young nobody. Subaltern in a foot regiment or something of that kind. Yes, poor chap was killed in a duel at Spa, just afterwards. Ugly business. They did say Kelso got some Belgian brute to insult his son-in-law in public and then paid him to spit him afterwards like a pigeon. The thing was hushed up but Kelso ate his chop alone at the Club for some time afterwards, I can tell you. Oh yes, it was a bad business. He brought her back with him but she'd never speak to him again and then she died as well before the year was out. So she left a son, did she? What's he like? If he's like his mother he must be a good-looking sort.

LORD HENRY: Oh, he is that.

LORD FERMOR: Long as he falls into proper hands. Should have a bit of money waiting for him if Kelso did the right thing by him.

LORD HENRY: I fancy he's well off. He has Selby, I know.

LORD FERMOR: She was one of the loveliest creatures I ever saw, Harry. Could have married anybody. She was romantic though. All the women in that family were. The men were a poor lot but the women were wonderful. By the way, Harry, talking about silly marriages, what's this humbug your father tells me about Dartmoor wanting to marry an American? Ain't English girls good enough for him?

LORD HENRY: It is rather fashionable to marry Americans just now, Uncle George.

LORD FERMOR: I'll back English women against the world.

LORD HENRY: The betting is on the Americans.

LORD FERMOR: They don't last, I'm told.

LORD HENRY: Long engagements exhaust them but they're capital at a steeplechase. They take things flying. I don't think Dartmoor has a chance.

LORD FERMOR: Who are her people? Has she got any?

LORD HENRY: American girls are as clever at concealing their parents as English women are at concealing their past.

LORD FERMOR: Pork packers, I suppose?

LORD HENRY: I hope so, Uncle George, for Dartmoor's sake. I'm told that pork packing is the most lucrative profession in America—after politics.

LORD FERMOR: Is she pretty?

LORD HENRY: She behaves as if she were beautiful. Most American women do. It's the secret of their charm.

LORD FERMOR: Why can't these American women stay in their own country? They're always telling us that it's the Woman's Paradise.

LORD HENRY: It appears to be. That is why, like Eve, they are so anxious to get out of it. Good-bye, Uncle George. Thanks for giving me the information. I always like to know everything about my new friends, and as little as possible about my old ones.

LORD FERMOR: Where are you lunching, Harry?

LORD HENRY: At Aunt Agatha's. I've asked myself and Mr. Gray. He's her latest protégé.

LORD FERMOR: Well, tell her from me not to bother me with any more of her charity appeals.

LORD HENRY: All right, Uncle George, I'll tell her but it won't have any effect. Philanthropic people lose all sense of humanity.

(LORD FERMOR *picks up his copy of* The Times *irritably and goes off, leaving his nephew alone with his thoughts. Presently, his* AUNT AGATHA *enters, chatting with her other guests. These are:* DORIAN; *the* DUCHESS OF HARLEY; SIR THOMAS BURDON, *a fashionable radical M.P.;* MR. ERSKINE, *an elderly gentleman.*

LADY AGATHA: Late as usual, Harry. You are a naughty boy. You know everyone, of course——

LORD HENRY: Of course.

DUCHESS OF HARLEY: We were talking about poor Dartmoor. Do you think he really will marry this fascinating young person?

LORD HENRY: I believe she's made up her mind to propose to him, Duchess.

LADY AGATHA: How dreadful! Really, someone should interfere.

SIR THOMAS: I am told, on excellent authority, that her father keeps an American dry-goods store.

DUCHESS OF HARLEY: Dry goods! What are American dry goods?

LORD HENRY: American novels.

LADY AGATHA: Don't mind him, my dear. He never means anything he says.

SIR THOMAS: When America was discovered——

DUCHESS OF HARLEY: I wish to goodness it had never been discovered at all! Really, our girls have no chance nowadays. It's most unfair.

MR. ERSKINE: Perhaps America has never been discovered at all. I'd say it had been merely *detected*.

DUCHESS OF HARLEY: Oh come, but I've seen specimens of the inhabitants and they dress well too. Most of them are extremely pretty. They get all their dresses in Paris. I wish I could afford to.

SIR THOMAS: They say when good Americans die they go to Paris.

DUCHESS OF HARLEY: And where do bad Americans go when they die?

LORD HENRY: They go to America.

SIR THOMAS: I'm afraid your nephew is being prejudiced. I have travelled all over it—with the encouragement of my directors. I can tell you: it is quite an education.

MR. ERSKINE: Must we really see Chicago in order to be educated? I don't feel up to it at all.

SIR THOMAS: Mr. Erskine sees the world from his bookshelves. We practical men like to see things, not read about them. The Americans are an extremely interesting people. They are absolutely reasonable. I can assure you there is no nonsense about the Americans.

LORD HENRY: I can stand brute force, but brute reason is quite unbearable. It is hitting below the intellect.

SIR THOMAS: I'm afraid I don't understand you.

MR. ERSKINE: But I think I do.

SIR THOMAS: Paradoxes are all very well in their way——

MR. ERSKINE: Was that a paradox? Perhaps it was. To test reality one must see it on a tightrope.

LADY AGATHA: How you men do argue! I'm sure I can never make out what you are talking about. Harry—I am quite vexed with you. Why are you trying to persuade our Mr. Gray to give up the East End?

LORD HENRY: I can sympathize with everything except suffering.

LADY AGATHA: Harry! The people in Whitechapel are utterly wretched and unhappy.

LORD HENRY: There is something terribly morbid in the cult of modern sympathy. I know a man with a toothache, for instance, should have mine. It can be a terrible pain but I can't stand him and I can't look at him. I only want to get away from him.

SIR THOMAS: You can't get away from the East End. It's a very important problem.

LORD HENRY: Quite. It is the problem of slavery. And we try to solve it by amusing the slaves.

SIR THOMAS: How would you change it then?

LORD HENRY: I don't propose to change anything in England. Except the weather. The nineteenth century has gone bankrupt. Through an over-expenditure on sympathy. My only investment has to be personal contemplation.

DUCHESS OF HARLEY: We do have terrible responsibilities——

LADY AGATHA: We certainly do!

LORD HENRY: The world takes itself too seriously. That is the key to original sin. If cavemen had known how to laugh, history would have been different.

DUCHESS OF HARLEY: How very comforting. I've always felt rather guilty when I came to see your dear aunt. You see, I take no interest in the East End either. In future I shall be able to look at her without blushing.

LORD HENRY: But yours is very becoming.

DUCHESS OF HARLEY: Only when one is young. When an old woman like myself blushes, it's not a good sign. I wish you could tell me how to become young again.

(*He thinks for a moment.*)

LORD HENRY: Can you remember any great error that you committed in your early days?

DUCHESS OF HARLEY: Only too many!

LORD HENRY: Then commit them over again. To get back one's youth, one has to repeat all one's follies.

DUCHESS OF HARLEY: What a delightful theory! I must put it into practice.

SIR THOMAS: A dangerous theory.

LORD HENRY: It is one of the great secrets. Nowadays, most people die of a sort of creeping common sense. It's only too late when they discover that the things one never really regrets are one's mistakes.

(*They all laugh.*)

DUCHESS OF HARLEY: How annoying! I must go. Lord Henry, you're quite delightful and dreadfully demoralizing. No, I must go, dear Agatha. Good-bye. (*To* LORD HENRY:) You must come and dine with us some night.

LORD HENRY: For you, I would throw over anybody.

DUCHESS OF HARLEY: That is very nice and very wrong of you. So mind you come Tuesday.

(*She goes out, followed by everyone except* LORD HENRY *and* DORIAN. MR. ERSKINE *pauses.*)

MR. ERSKINE: You talk books away. Why don't you write one?

LORD HENRY: I am too fond of reading books to care to write them, Mr. Erskine. I should like to write a novel, certainly. But there is no public in England for anything except newspapers, reviews, primers and encyclopaedias. Of all the people in the world, the English have the least sense of literature.

MR. ERSKINE: I'm afraid you are right. I used to have literary ambitions myself but I have given them up long ago. The generation into which I was born was tedious. Some day, when you are tired of London, come down to Treadly. And now I'm due at the Athenaeum. It is the hour when we sleep there.

LORD HENRY: All of you, Mr. Erskine?

MR. ERSKINE: Forty of us in forty armchairs!

(*He goes out.*)

LORD HENRY (*to* DORIAN): I am going to the Park.

DORIAN: Stay and talk with me.

LORD HENRY: I thought you had promised to go and see Basil Hallward?

DORIAN: I'd sooner be with you.

LORD HENRY: I have talked quite enough for today. All I want to do is to look at life. But just as you wish.

(*They go and sit in another part of the stage.* LORD HENRY *takes out a cigarette and lights it.*)

DORIAN: Tell me about your wife.

LORD HENRY: Tell you what?

DORIAN: I saw you together at *Lohengrin* the other night.

LORD HENRY: Do I take it that you are already interested in the practicality of marriage?

DORIAN: Yes. I am. Very much so.

LORD HENRY: Indeed? You must tell me about it.

DORIAN: If you remember, I was asking about your own wife.

LORD HENRY: Victoria? She's a curious woman. A mania for going to church and her dresses always look as if they have been designed and arranged and put on in the middle of a tempest. She's usually in love with somebody, and as her passion is hardly ever returned, she has managed to keep most of her illusions. She does try to look picturesque but only ends up looking untidy. Marriage . . . never marry a woman with straw-coloured hair, Dorian.

DORIAN: Why, Harry?

LORD HENRY: They're so sentimental.

DORIAN: But I like people to be sentimental.

LORD HENRY: My advice to you is, Dorian: don't marry at all. Men marry because they are tired. Women, because they're curious. Both are disappointed.

DORIAN: My life: is not one of your aphorisms, Harry. I think I deserve better of you than that.

(*Pause.*)

35

LORD HENRY: Who are you in love with?

DORIAN: An actress.

LORD HENRY: That's rather a commonplace début.

DORIAN: You wouldn't say so if you saw her.

LORD HENRY: Who is she?

DORIAN: Well, her name, if that's what you mean, is Sibyl Vane.

LORD HENRY: Never heard of her.

DORIAN: Nobody has. But they will do. She's a genius.

LORD HENRY: My dear boy, no woman is a genius. They never have anything to say, but they say it quite well.

Women represent the triumph of matter over mind, just as men represent the triumph of mind over morals. There are only two kinds of women, the plain and the coloured. The plain are very useful. And if you want to keep a reputation for respectability, you have merely to ask them round to supper. As long as a woman can look ten years younger than her daughter, she is perfectly satisfied. And as for conversation, there are only five women in London worth talking to, anyway. And two of those can't be admitted into decent society. Still, tell me about your female genius. How long have you known her?

DORIAN: You can't be right in that about women.

LORD HENRY: Never mind that. How long have you known her?

DORIAN: About three weeks.

LORD HENRY: And how did you come across her?

DORIAN: I'll tell you, Harry—but you must listen and listen properly. I think, a little while ago, it might never have happened at all . . . I had been walking about London, just walking. Just looking and watching, at everyone I passed or who passed me . . . some of them seemed fascinating—simply to see. Some of the others terrified me and I'd hurry on instead of staying. I don't know what on earth I was expecting. Anyway, one night I was out in the direction of your Aunt Agatha's famous East End. Well, about half-past eight, I passed by an absurd little theatre, all flaring gas jets and playbills. Standing outside was a hideous Jew, in the most amazing waistcoat I think I've ever seen. 'Have a box, my Lord?' he said. And he took this vile cigar out of his

36

mouth and tipped his hat at me with what seemed like a—a gorgeous servility. There was something about him at that moment that took my fancy. He was such a genuine *monster*. I know you'll laugh at me but he managed to get me to do it. But if I hadn't —my dear Harry—if I hadn't, I should have missed the greatest thing that's happened to me in my life . . . I knew you would laugh.

LORD HENRY: I'm not laughing, Dorian. At least I'm not laughing at you. But you shouldn't say it's the greatest thing in your life. You will always be loved. And you, you will always be in love with the idea of love itself. (*Less seriously.*) A grand passion is the privilege of people who have nothing to do. That is the one use of the idle classes of any country. I just ask you not to be afraid. There are ravishing things in store for you. This is merely the beginning.

DORIAN: Then I *am* shallow.

LORD HENRY: My dear boy, the people who love only once in their lives are really the shallow people. They call it loyalty or fidelity. I call it the lethargy of custom. Or the lack of imagination. Faithfulness is to the emotional life what consistency is to the life of the intellect—simply a confession of failures. Faithfulness! The passion for property is in it. Oh, Dorian, there are many things we would all throw away if we were not afraid that someone else might pick them up. But you'd better go on.

DORIAN: So there I found myself sitting in a horrid little private box and a grotesque drop-scene staring me in the face. I looked out from behind the curtain at the house. It was a pretty depressing affair, you know, all cupids and cornu-copias, like a cheap wedding cake. The gallery and pit were fairly full but the stalls were almost empty and scarcely anybody in what I suppose they call the dress circle. There were women selling oranges and ginger beer without end, to say nothing of a deafening sound of nuts being chomped on.

LORD HENRY: The familiar, palmy days of British Drama.

DORIAN: I looked at the programme and it turned out that the play that night was *Romeo and Juliet*. I can't say I was relishing the idea of being confronted with Shakespeare in this odd hole-in-the-ground place. But by this time I'd got a bit interested in the atmosphere, such as it was, and I thought I'd see out a bit of the first act. Oh yes, and there was a dreadful orchestra presided over by a young Hebrew, sitting at a cracked piano. That nearly drove me out but then they took up the drop finally and the play started—in its own peculiar way. I didn't pay much attention to it. I looked at the audience more than the stage. Romeo was like an old beer-barrel and Mercutio was played by the local comedian just in order to put in his favourite gags, as far as I can make out. And then Juliet came on . . . Harry, she was the loveliest thing I have ever seen in my life. You said to me once that pathos left you unmoved but that beauty—something merely beautiful—could fill your eyes with tears. I tell you, Harry: I could hardly see this girl. For the mist of tears that came across my line of sight. And when she spoke—her voice. I've never heard anything like it. I can't forget it, the evening—I can't forget *her*. She's everything in life to me. I go and see her night after night.

LORD HENRY: I see.

(*Pause.*)

DORIAN: Ordinary women never appeal to one's imagination. They are limited to their century. No proper excitement ever transfigures them. One knows their mind as easily as one recognizes their hats. They are always to be found. There is no mystery in any of them. They ride in the Park in the morning and chatter at tea parties in the afternoon. They have their stereotype style and their fashionable manner.

LORD HENRY: Oh yes, they're quite obvious.

DORIAN: Henry—why didn't you tell me what it is: loving an actress?

LORD HENRY: Because I have loved so many of them, Dorian.

DORIAN: Now you make me wish I hadn't told you about Sibyl Vane.

LORD HENRY: You couldn't have helped telling me, Dorian. You will tell me everything you do all your life.

DORIAN: Yes, Harry, I believe that's true. I *do* tell you things. I think if I ever did a crime for instance, I would come and tell you. You might understand.

LORD HENRY: People like you don't commit crimes, Dorian. But I'm obliged for the compliment, all the same. And now tell me—reach me the matches, like a good chap—what are your actual relations with Sibyl Vane?

DORIAN: What do you mean by asking such a question?

LORD HENRY: It's only the sacred things that are worth touching, Dorian.

(*Pause.*)

But why should you be annoyed? I suppose she will belong to you some day. When one is in love, one always begins by deceiving oneself and always ends by deceiving others. That is what is known in the world as romance. You do know her?

DORIAN: Of course I know her. On the first night I was at the theatre, the old Jew came round to the box after the performance and asked me backstage to introduce me to her. I declined.

LORD HENRY: So when did you first speak to Miss Sibyl Vane?

DORIAN: After the third evening. She'd been playing Rosalind and I couldn't help myself. I'd thrown her some flowers and she looked up at me. At least, I thought she did. The old boy was still persistent. He seemed set on taking me round, so I said yes. It was curious, my not wanting to meet her the first time, wasn't it?

LORD HENRY: No. I don't think so.

DORIAN: Why?

LORD HENRY: I'll tell you another time. At this moment I want to know about the girl.

DORIAN: Sibyl? There's something of a child about her. But far, far more than that. In the way people usually mean. The man wanted to talk about her past but I wasn't interested.

LORD HENRY: You were quite right. There's invariably something mean about other people's tragedies.

DORIAN: Sibyl is the only thing I care about now. Every night of

my life I go to see her. And every night she's more
marvellous.

(*Pause.*)

LORD HENRY: That is the reason, I suppose, that you never dine
with me now. I thought you must have some curious
romance on hand. You have. But it's not quite what I
expected.

DORIAN: I get hungry simply from her presence. I think of
what's concealed inside that small strange body.

LORD HENRY: You can dine with me tonight, Dorian, can't you?

DORIAN: Tonight she's Rosalind.

LORD HENRY: And tomorrow night?

DORIAN: Juliet again . . .

LORD HENRY: When is she Sibyl Vane?

DORIAN: Never.

LORD HENRY: I congratulate you. So: what do you propose to do?

DORIAN: I want you and Basil to come with me some night and
see her in the theatre. I am not at all apprehensive. You'll
see what I mean at once. Then we'll get her out of the old
boy's hands. She's contracted to him for three years or
something, but I can buy him out. And when all that is
settled, I'll take a West End theatre and bring her out
properly. She'll do for the world what she's done for me.

LORD HENRY: That would be impossible, my dear friend.

DORIAN: Oh, she will. She hasn't merely got art, a consummate
art-instinct in her, but she has personality. And a unique
one. You've often told me yourself that it is personalities
and not principles that move the age.

LORD HENRY: Let me see. Today is Tuesday. Let us fix
tomorrow. When she is playing Juliet.

DORIAN: All right. The Bristol at eight o'clock. And I'll pick up
Basil. Poor Basil. I haven't seen him for a week at least. It's
rather awful of me as he sent me my portrait in a most
wonderful frame, especially designed by himself. I'm—to
tell you the truth—a fraction jealous of the picture for being
a whole month younger than me, but I must admit I'm
delighted with it. Perhaps *you* had better write to him. I
don't want to see him alone. Everything he says irritates me

a bit. He will give *advice*.

LORD HENRY: People do tend to give away what they need most themselves.

DORIAN: Oh, I'm very fond of Basil but he does have a touch of the philistine. You know what I mean?

LORD HENRY: Basil, my dear boy, puts everything that is charming or interesting in him into his work. The consequence is that he has nothing left for life but his prejudices, his principles and his commonsense. The only artists I have ever known, who are personally delightful, are bad artists. Good artists exist simply in what they make and consequently are perfectly uninteresting in what they are. A great poet, a really great poet, is the most unpoetical of all creatures but in theory bad poets are absolutely fascinating. They live the poetry they cannot write. The others write the poetry that they dare not realize.

DORIAN: Do you think that is really so, Harry?

(*He takes up his hat and cane with easy enjoyment.*)

I suppose it is—if you say so. And now I'm off. Don't forget about tomorrow. Good-bye.

(*He goes out to leave,* LORD HENRY's *eyes following him.*)

SCENE III

A front cloth of the period clatters down in front of the main set. In front of this is a small simple dressing-table, a chair and screen. Seated at the dressing-table is SIBYL VANE *in her Shakespearean costume. With her are her mother,* MRS. VANE, *and her young brother* JAMES.

SIBYL: Mother, I'm so happy. I *am*, James. You must see that? You do feel it? You do feel it?

MRS. VANE: Happy! I don't know about that. I don't know about *happy*! The thing that makes me happy is to see you on those boards, Sibyl. That's what you've got to think about. Mr. Isaacs has been very good to us.

SIBYL: Oh, money, Mother! There must be more than that.

MRS. VANE: Mr. Isaacs has advanced us fifty pounds to pay off our debts *and* to get a proper outfit for James here. There's no getting round that, Sibyl. Fifty pounds is a very great deal. And Mr. Isaacs has been more than considerate.

SIBYL: I hate everything about him.

MRS. VANE: I don't know how we'd manage without him.

SIBYL: We don't want him and we don't need him. Something else has come into our lives. And I just love him.

MRS. VANE: A great deal that means.

SIBYL: Then why does he feel the same way about me? I know why I love him. I love him because he's like what things should be. What is it that he sees in me? I don't even feel humble. I feel proud, Mother, yes, terribly proud. How did you love my father then? Forgive me. Don't look that way. I must be as happy as you ever were. Just let it go on!

MRS. VANE: My child, you are much too young to think of these things and what they entail. What do you know of this young man? Not even his name. Oh, it all couldn't have happened at a worse time! What with James off to Australia—with so much to occupy me, I must say I do think you could have shown a bit more consideration. I dare say he's rich but what does that mean?

SIBYL: Don't say these things.

(*She kisses her mother.*)

JAMES: You might keep some of that for me I think, Sibyl.

SIBYL: You don't really like it, Jim. You know you don't.

JAMES: Come out with me afterwards. I shouldn't think I'll ever see this London of yours again. I'm sure I don't want to.

MRS. VANE: You shouldn't talk like that.

JAMES: Why not? I mean it.

MRS. VANE: It's morbid, anyway. When you come back from Australia you'll be *somebody*. There's nothing like what you call Society out there—at least what I call Society. So when you've made your packet you can come back and take your proper place here in London.

JAMES: Society! I can't think that's very interesting. I should just like to make a bit of money and get you and Sibyl away from the stage. I hate everything about it.

SIBYL: Oh, Jim! How little you do understand. You're an old, young silly! Wait a moment while I change.

(*She goes behind the screen. The* MOTHER *and* SON *look at each other without much life in them.*)

JAMES: Are my things ready?

MRS. VANE: Quite ready.

(*Pause.*)

Well, I hope you'll take to the sea, James. Or, at least that it takes to you. You will remember that it's at your own choice. You could have been a solicitor if I had my way. Solicitors are a very respected class of people. In the country they very often dine with the very best families.

JAMES: I hate offices and I hate class. But you're quite right. I've chosen my own life. All I say to you is: keep a watch over Sibyl. Don't let her come to any harm. Mother, you've got to watch over her.

MRS. VANE: You do talk very funny sometimes, James. Of course I'll watch over Sibyl. What else do you think I'll do?

JAMES: I hear there's a gentleman comes every night to the theatre and comes back here to talk to her. Is that right? Well, what about it?

MRS. VANE: You are talking about things you simply don't understand, James. We are accustomed to receiving a great deal of attention in the profession. Which is something you've never really understood. And many don't or won't. It used to happen to me all the time. That was when acting was really understood. As for Sibyl, I've no way of knowing whether her present attachment is serious or not. All I do know is that the young man in question is a perfect gentleman. He's always most polite to me. He has all the *air* of being very rich indeed. And the flowers he sends are lovely.

JAMES: But you don't know his name?

MRS. VANE: No. He hasn't yet revealed his real name. I confess that. I think it's quite romantic of him. I'd say he's probably a member of the aristocracy.

JAMES: Just watch over her, Mother. You watch over her.

MRS. VANE: Why are you talking to me like this? I've always

looked after Sibyl from first to last. Of course, if he is a worthy gentleman, there's no reason why she shouldn't contract an alliance with him. Especially if he's one of the aristocracy. And he has all the appearance of it, I must say. It'd be the most brilliant marriage for Sibyl. They'd make quite a couple. His looks are really *remarkable*. Everybody notices them.

(SIBYL *comes in from behind the screen.*)

SIBYL: Oh, how serious you both look! What's up with the two of you now?

JAMES: Nothing. Good-bye, Mother.

MRS. VANE: Good-bye, son. Take care in all that wet weather.

(*They kiss rather awkwardly.* MRS. VANE *turns with relief back to* SIBYL *and embraces her.*)

See you later, Sibyl dear. I'll get a drop for both of us around the corner.

(*She goes out.*)

SIBYL: Everything will be all right for both of us. You'll come back from Australia with everything you want and I'll be here in London with everything I want. We'll all be together. And that's what life will be like. . . . Jim, you're not listening to a word I'm saying. I've just set out the most exquisite plans for both of us. Say something to me— please.

JAMES: What do you want me to say?

SIBYL: Oh—just that you will be a good boy and not forget us.

(*He holds her shoulders and looks at her in the mirror.*)

JAMES: You're more likely to forget me than I am to forget you, Sibyl.

SIBYL: What do you mean?

(*She is disturbed.*)

JAMES: You have a new friend, I hear. Who is he? Why haven't you told me about him? Does he mean you any good?

SIBYL: Stop it! You're not to say anything against him. I love him.

JAMES: Someone whose name you don't even know. Who is he? I've a right to know.

SIBYL: If only you could see him, you'd think him the most

44

wonderful person in the world. Some day you will—when you come back from Australia. You'll like him so much. Everybody does. And I . . . love him. I just wish you could come to the theatre tonight. He's going to be there and I'm playing Juliet. What about that, to be in love and play Juliet! I shall probably frighten the company to death. To be in love is to *surpass* oneself. Poor old Mr. Isaacs will be shouting 'genius' to all his cronies at the bar. Our proverbs want rewriting. They were made in winter. Now it's summer or springtime or something. I don't know who said it. Perhaps *I* did. Just then.

JAMES: He wants to enslave you.

SIBYL: I shudder at the thought of being free.

JAMES: I want you to protect yourself from him.

SIBYL: I see him and I worship him.

JAMES: Sibyl, you *are* mad about him.

SIBYL: Dear Jim, you are leaving me when I am happier than I've ever been before. Life's been hard for both of us. But it will be different now. You are going to a new world and mine's already found.

JAMES: Well, mine isn't. And I don't believe in yours. Although I wish to God I did.

SIBYL: Love makes people good.

JAMES: You believe that? I'm going now. But I tell you: if he ever does you any wrong—I shall kill him.

FADE

SCENE IV

Main set. BASIL HALLWARD *is studying one of his paintings as* LORD HENRY *enters.*

LORD HENRY: I suppose you've heard the news?

BASIL: No, what is it? As long as it's not about politics.

LORD HENRY: Dorian Gray is engaged to be married.

BASIL: Engaged to be married! I don't believe it.

LORD HENRY: It's perfectly true.

BASIL: To whom?

LORD HENRY: Some little actress or other.

BASIL: I don't believe it. Dorian is far too sensible.

LORD HENRY: Dorian is far too wise not to do foolish things now and then, my dear Basil.

BASIL: Marriage is hardly a thing one can do now and then, Harry.

LORD HENRY: Except in America. But I didn't say he was married. I said he was engaged to be married. There is a great difference.

BASIL: But one's only got to think of Dorian's birth and position and wealth. To marry a girl like that is unthinkable.

LORD HENRY: If you want to make him marry this girl, tell him just that. He's quite sure to do it then. Whenever a man does a thoroughly stupid thing, it's so often from the noblest motives.

BASIL: Well, I hope she is all right. I'd hate to see Dorian tied to some vile creature who might degrade his very own nature and soften up his intellect.

LORD HENRY: Oh, she's better than all right or even good—she's beautiful. Dorian says she's beautiful and he's not often wrong about that kind of thing. You know, your portrait of him has quickened his appreciation altogether. Particularly about people's personal appearances. But that's not the only effect it's had on him. Anyhow, we, you and I, are going to see her tonight. That is, if Dorian doesn't forget all about it in his delirium.

BASIL: Are you serious?

LORD HENRY: I think I should be miserable if I were ever more serious than I am at this moment.

BASIL: But you can't possibly approve of this business. It's an infatuation, surely.

LORD HENRY: I never approve or disapprove of anything now. It's an absurd attitude to take towards life. Dorian Gray falls in love with a beautiful girl who happens to play Juliet and proposes to marry her. Why not? If he wedded Messalina, he'd be nontheless interesting. You know, I'm not a

champion of marriage. The real drawback to that institution
is that it makes one unselfish. And unselfish people are
colourless. They lack individuality. Still, there are certain
temperaments that marriage makes more complex. They
retain their egotism and add it to a lot of other egos. They
are forced to have more than one life and so become more
highly organized. Besides, every experience has great value,
and, whatever one may say against marriage, it is certainly
an experience. I, for one, hope that Dorian will make this
girl his wife, passionately adore her for six months and then
suddenly become fascinated by someone else. It would be a
remarkable study.

BASIL: You know you don't mean a single word of all that. If
Dorian Gray's life were spoiled, no one would be more
sorry than you.

LORD HENRY (*laughing*): I am trying to be optimistic. The basis of
optimism is sheer terror. We praise the banker in order that
he may let us overdraw our account. Or even try to find
good qualities in the burglar in the hope that he may leave
our property alone. Oh, I mean everything I've said. I have
nothing but the greatest contempt for optimism. As for what
you call a spoiled life, no life is spoiled except those whose
growth is arrested. If you set out to mar a nature, you've
merely to reform it. As for marriage, I agree with you that
would be silly. But there are other more interesting bonds
between men and women. Why don't you let Dorian tell you
for himself?

(*Before he has finished this sentence,* DORIAN *has entered.*)

DORIAN: Harry! My dear Basil! You must both congratulate me!
I've never been so happy. Of course it's sudden and all that
but all the really delightful things are. It seems to be one
thing I've been looking for all my life.

BASIL: I hope you'll always be happy like that, Dorian. I don't
know that I can quite forgive you for not coming to let me
know about your engagement. You told Harry.

LORD HENRY: And I don't forgive you for being late. Come, let's
sit down and you can tell us how it all happened.

DORIAN: There isn't really very much. After I left you yesterday

47

evening, Harry, I had some dinner at that little Italian restaurant in Rupert Street you introduced me to and went down at eight o'clock to the theatre. Sibyl was playing Rosalind. Of course the scenery was dreadful and the Orlando absurd. But Sibyl! You should have seen her! As for her performance—well, you'll see her tonight. She's simply a born artist. I sat in that awful box—and I forgot that I was in London. I forgot I was in the nineteenth century. (*He comes out of a kind of reverie.*) Of course our engagement's a dead secret. She hasn't even told her own mother and I don't know what my guardian will say. Not that I care . . . She flung herself on her knees and kissed my hands. I shouldn't be telling you all this but I can't help it.

(*Pause.*)

LORD HENRY: At what particular point did you mention the word 'marriage', Dorian? And what did she say in reply? Or perhaps you've forgotten all about it?

DORIAN: My dear Harry, I didn't treat it as a business transaction. And I suppose I didn't make any formal proposal.

LORD HENRY: And what did you say then?

DORIAN: That I loved her of course. She said—oh, something about not being worthy to be my wife. Something like that.

LORD HENRY: Women are wonderfully practical. Much more practical than we are. In situations of that kind we often forget to say anything about marriage and they always remind us.

BASIL: Leave it alone, Harry. You're only annoying Dorian. He isn't like the rest of us. He'd never bring misery on anyone. He is too fine for that.

LORD HENRY: Dorian is never annoyed with me. I asked the question for the best reason possible. For the only reason, indeed, that excuses anyone for asking any question. Simple curiosity. I have a theory that it is always the women who propose to us and not we who propose to the women. Except, of course, in middle-class life. But then the middle classes are not modern.

DORIAN: I don't mind. It's impossible to be angry with you.

When you see Sibyl Vane, you'll know that anyone who could consider wronging her would be a monster without a heart at all. I can't understand how anyone can want to degrade the thing he loves. I never have . . . I love Sibyl Vane . . . I want to worship her and I want the world to do the same. What is marriage? An irrevocable vow? You make fun of it for that. Well, don't! It's because it's irrevocable that I want to make it. Her trust makes me faithful, just as I know that her belief will make me good. When I am with her, I regret everything else I've ever learned. I become quite different from what you've known me to be. I'm changed. The simplest touch of her hand makes me forget you and everyone else and their poisonous theories.

LORD HENRY: Which are?

DORIAN: Oh, theories about life, about love, your theories about pleasure. *All* theories.

LORD HENRY: Pleasure is the only thing worth having a theory about. But I am afraid I can't claim that as my own. It belongs to nature, not to me. Pleasure is nature's test, her code of approval. When we are happy we are always good, but when we are good we are not always happy.

BASIL: Ah! But what do you mean by good?

DORIAN: Yes, what do you mean?

LORD HENRY: To be good is to be in harmony with oneself. Discord is to be forced to be in harmony with others. One's own life—that's an important thing. Individualism is the highest aim. Whereas modern morality consists in accepting the standards of one's age, I believe that for any man of culture to accept the standard of his age is the grossest immorality.

BASIL: But, surely, if one lives merely for oneself, one pays a terrible price for doing so.

LORD HENRY: Yes, we are overcharged for everything nowadays. It seems to me that the real tragedy of the poor is that they can afford nothing but self-denial. Beautiful sins, like beautiful things, are the privilege of the rich.

BASIL: There are other ways of having to pay apart from money.

DORIAN: What sort of ways?

BASIL: Oh, I don't know. Remorse? Suffering? The consciousness of degradation.

LORD HENRY: My dear fellow, medieval art has its charm but medieval emotions are out of date. Believe me, no civilized man ever regrets a pleasure and no uncivilized man ever really knows what a pleasure is.

DORIAN: I know what it is. It's to adore someone.

LORD HENRY: That is certainly better than being adored. It's a downright nuisance. When women worship someone, they're always bothering them to do something for them.

DORIAN: I should have thought that whatever they ask for they've already given first. They create love in one's nature. They've a right to demand it back.

BASIL: Quite true.

LORD HENRY: Nothing is ever quite true.

DORIAN: Well—*this* is. Can't you admit, Harry, that women give men the very essence of themselves?

LORD HENRY: Possibly. But they invariably want it back in such very small change. That's the worry. Women, some witty Frenchman once put it, inspire us with a desire to do masterpieces and always prevent us from carrying them out.

DORIAN: I don't know why I like you at all.

LORD HENRY: You will always like me, Dorian. Now, after all that, you must have a cigarette. A cigarette is the perfect type of a perfect pleasure. It is delicious and it leaves one unsatisfied. What more can one ask? Yes, Dorian, you will always be fond of me. I represent to you all the sins you never have the courage to commit.

DORIAN: What utter rubbish you do talk, Harry! Come on! Let's get down to the theatre. When Sibyl comes on the stage, then it will be your turn to find a new ideal of life. She may represent something that even you have never experienced.

LORD HENRY: I have known everything but I'm always ready for new emotion. I'm afraid, however, that, for me at any rate, there's no such thing. Still, your wonderful girl may be thrilling at the very least. I love acting—so much more real than life. Let's go, then, Dorian. You come with me. Sorry,

Basil, but there's only room for two in the brougham. You can follow in a hansom.

(*The two men get up and put on their coats and make their way out.* BASIL *sits alone in a chair, silent and preoccupied. After a while, he gets up and follows them off.*)

SCENE V

Front cloth descends, as before, in front of the main set with the same furnishings. MRS. VANE *is busying herself with* SIBYL'*s costumes. There is a knock on the door and she calls out.*

MRS. VANE: Come in.

(*The door opens and some desultory applause can be heard from the stage together with one or two whistles. In come* DORIAN GRAY, LORD HENRY *and* BASIL HALLWARD.)

MRS. VANE: Why, good evening, sir. We knew you were out front. I'm afraid she's not off yet.

DORIAN: I know.

MRS. VANE: She's expecting you.

DORIAN: Could you leave us?

MRS. VANE: But I've got to help her with her costumes and——

DORIAN: That won't be necessary. These gentlemen are not staying and I shall be gone soon. Would you please leave us?

MRS. VANE: Now?

DORIAN: Now.

(*She looks at the three men, rather alarmed, and passes between them muttering out of the dressing-room.*)

BASIL: Poor woman.

DORIAN: I dare say I shall see the play through. I'm awfully sorry I made you both waste an evening. I apologize.

LORD HENRY: My dear Dorian, I should think Miss Vane was probably ill. We'll come some other night.

DORIAN: I wish she were ill. But she's simply callous and cold. She's altered entirely. Last night I thought she was a great artist. This evening she's merely commonplace and mediocre.

51

BASIL: Don't talk like that about anyone you love, Dorian.
Love is a more wonderful thing than art.

LORD HENRY: They are both simply forms of imitation.

BASIL: Don't pay any attention to him, Dorian. I beg of you. I
can understand what you mean. And I believe in her.
Anyone you love must be marvellous and any girl that has
the effect you describe to us must be very extraordinary and
unique. To have produced that effect in *you*—that is worth
doing in itself. If she can create a sense of beauty and worth
in people whose lives are sordid and ugly, she can strip
them of all kinds of every selfishness and things and perhaps
even give them a cult of tears they never had before. That
makes her worthy of your adoration. And of the adoration of
all of us. Your idea of marriage is quite right. I didn't think
so at first but now I admit it, freely. Sibyl Vane was made
for you. Without her you would probably have been
incomplete for the rest of your life.

DORIAN: Thanks, Basil. I knew you would at least try to
understand.

(*Pause.*)

LORD HENRY: I think we should go. And you too, Dorian. It is
not good for one's morals to see bad acting. Besides, I don't
suppose you will want to see your wife act much longer. So
what does it matter if she plays Juliet like a wooden doll?
She is very lovely indeed, and if she knows as little about
life as she does about acting, she will be a delightful
experience. There are only two kinds of people who are
really fascinating—people who know absolutely everything
and people who know absolutely nothing. Good heavens, my
dear boy, don't look so tragic! Come to the club with Basil
and myself. We'll smoke and drink to the beauty of Sibyl
Vane. She *is* beautiful. What more can you want?

DORIAN: Go away, Harry. Please take him with you, Basil.

BASIL: Let's go.

(*The two men look at* DORIAN *and then go. From the stage
comes a sound of a few groans and jeers. He goes over to the
dressing-room table and looks into the mirror. After a while,*
SIBYL *appears alone at the door. She looks elated.*)

SIBYL: I acted so badly tonight, Dorian.

DORIAN: Horribly! You were dreadful. Are you ill or something? Haven't you any idea what it was? You obviously have no idea of what *I* went through.

SIBYL: Dorian, you should have understood. But you understand now, don't you?

DORIAN: Understand what?

SIBYL: Why I was so bad tonight. Why I shall always be bad. Why I shall never be any good again.

DORIAN: You are ill. When you are ill you shouldn't go on. You make yourself ridiculous. My friends were bored. I was bored.

SIBYL: Dorian, before I knew you, acting was the one reality of my life. I only lived for the theatre, I thought it was all true what went on. And then you came—oh, my dearest, and you freed my self from all that. *You* taught me reality. Tonight, for the first time in my life, I saw the hollowness of everything I devoted myself to. You'd made me understand what love really is. My love, I've grown sick of shadows. You are more to me than any art could ever be. It all went. I went on thinking I was going to be wonderful. I found I could be *nothing*. Suddenly it dawned on me what it all meant. The knowledge opened out to me right in the middle of all that hissing and noise—and I smiled to myself. What did any of them know? Take me away, Dorian—take me away with you where we can be quite alone. I hate the stage. I might mimic badly a passion I don't feel but I can't mimic one that burns me like this . . . You see what a blasphemy it would be: to play at being in love?

DORIAN: You have killed all that.

(*She laughs a little and goes to stroke his hair, then kneels beside him but he draws away, as if she were utterly distasteful to be near.*)

Yes, you killed it. You used to stir my imagination. Now you don't even stir my curiosity. In fact, you produce no effect on me at all. I loved you because you were a marvellous thing. Because you had genius and intellect. Because you seemed to give substance to all things I'd ever

53

dreamed of. You've thrown that away. You are shallow and stupid. My God! What could I have been thinking of! You *are* a nothing. I'll never see you again, I'll never think of you, I'll even forget your name. I only wish I'd never laid eyes on you. What little you know about love if you say it mars your art. Without your art you're nothing. I'd have made you famous, splendid, magnificent. You'd have been worshipped by everyone and my name would have been on you. What are you now?

SIBYL: You're not serious, Dorian! You are acting.

DORIAN: Acting! I'll leave that to you. You do it so well.

(*She rushes across the room and tries to touch his arm but he thrusts her back.*)

Never touch me again.

(*She throws herself at his feet hardly able to speak.*)

SIBYL: Dorian, Dorian, don't leave me. I'm so sorry I didn't act well. I was thinking of you all the time. But I *will* try— believe me, I will. It came so suddenly across me . . . all my love. I'll work hard. I'll improve. Don't be cruel to me because I love you better than anything in the world. After all, it's only once I haven't pleased you. But you are quite right, Dorian. I should have shown myself more of an artist. More. It was foolish of me; and yet I couldn't help it. Oh, don't leave me! Don't leave me.

(DORIAN *looks down at her sobbing on the floor at his feet.*)

DORIAN: There is always something ridiculous about the emotions of people whom one has ceased to love. I am going now. I don't wish to be unkind but I can't see you again. You have disappointed me. That is all.

(*He goes out.*)

FADE

SCENE VI

The front cloth rolls up and the furniture and props are struck.
DORIAN GRAY *comes into the main set taking off his coat and hat and placing his cane on a table. He looks around the room and at all the exotic objects in it, the tapestries, the paintings, the carpets, and so on. One or two objects he picks up. He then goes to the portrait of himself painted by* BASIL HALLWARD. *He takes it up from the floor and goes over to the window where he places it so that he can see the image more clearly. He stares at it as if it were puzzling in some way. Then he goes over to a chair, sits down and stares at it. He gets up again to look out of a window and looks out into the darkness. Under his breath he whispers the name 'Sibyl'. His attention is caught by the picture again and he goes back to his vantage point and sits staring at it.*

Act Two

The scene is the same and DORIAN *is still staring at the portrait. Now,
however, it is in a more prominent position on the stage and covered with
an old gilt Spanish leather screen. He puts down an elaborately produced yellow book which is open on his lap and moves over to the
covered portrait. Just as it seems as if he might remove the screen, his
valet,* VICTOR, *appears.* DORIAN *shivers and returns to his seat.*

VICTOR: You rang, *monsieur?*

DORIAN: No, of course I didn't ring. Oh yes, I did.

VICTOR: It is too cold for *monsieur?* Shall I shut the window?

DORIAN: No, I'm not cold. Yes—shut it.

    (VICTOR *does so.*)

VICTOR: Is there anything else, *monsieur?*

DORIAN: What? Oh, you did see that Miss Vane got my letter?

VICTOR: I delivered it myself, *monsieur.* Although the house was
    very difficult to find.

DORIAN: Did you give it to her personally?

VICTOR: No, *monsieur,* but I gave it to someone who called
    herself the landlady. I think she was a little cross at being
    disturbed but she promised me that it would be delivered
    into the right hands.

DORIAN: Very well. I am not at home to anyone, Victor, except to
    Miss Vane.

VICTOR: And Lord Henry, *monsieur?*

DORIAN: What about him? I told you I'm only at home to Miss
    Vane. Do you remember that? Miss Sibyl Vane.

VICTOR: It's only that his man sent round a letter first thing this
    morning, *monsieur.* It was marked urgent and I left it on
    your breakfast tray.

DORIAN: Oh yes, I remember it. Well, it can't be that important.

I'll read it later. Now, don't forget to let her in at once. That's all.

VICTOR: Yes, *monsieur*.

(DORIAN *waits for his valet to leave. When he has done so,* he *gets up and locks the doors. He listens for a moment and then returns to the portrait, carefully lifting the screen from it and standing back to gaze at it. What he sees clearly horrifies him.*

As he goes back to his chair to stare at the portrait, there is a doorbell ring offstage. He ignores it and continues to look at the picture, then gets up and examines it in detail, almost like a dealer might.

After a while, there is a sound of voices including that of LORD HENRY *outside the door. This is followed by loud and persistent knocking at* DORIAN's *room. Unhurriedly, he goes on surveying the portrait with great scrutiny. Then, in the same slow fashion, he replaces the screen, unlocks the doors, finally coming to the one being pounded on by* LORD HENRY, *who enters at once.*)

LORD HENRY: My dear boy, I had to see you. Forgive me but the thought of you shutting yourself up in this way—I'm so very sorry about it all for you, Dorian. But you mustn't sit here on your own, thinking about it.

DORIAN: You mean—about Sibyl Vane?

LORD HENRY: Well, of course. It's quite dreadful, from every point of view. But you mustn't—you mustn't—think of it as *your* fault. Tell me, did you stay with her long after we both left you?

DORIAN: A while.

LORD HENRY: I knew you would. Was there a scene?

DORIAN: I was brutal. Yes, brutal and unforgivable. But that's over now. I'm not even sorry now for what happened. Except for the pain I caused. At least, it has taught me to know myself.

LORD HENRY: Ah, Dorian, I'm glad you can look on it like that— even now. I thought I'd find you in despair.

DORIAN: That is all over. I am perfectly—as happy as I shall ever be. For one thing, I know what conscience is. And don't swear at that any more. Not in front of me, anyway. I can see through it. And I do—well, I would like to be good. As much as I can. I can't face the idea of my inner self being hideous any longer.

LORD HENRY: A very charming basis for ethics. Well done! But how do you propose to begin this moral regime?

DORIAN: By marrying Sibyl Vane.

LORD HENRY: Marrying—Sibyl Vane! But, my dear Dorian——

DORIAN: Yes, Henry, I know what you're going to say: something tiresomely sarcastic about marriage. Well, don't. And not to me ever again. I've written again to Sibyl since last night—that ridiculous night—and I've asked her again to marry me. If she'll have me. My mind's made up. She's going to be my wife.

LORD HENRY: Your wife! Dorian. My letter—didn't you get it? I sent the note down myself this morning. By my own man.

DORIAN: Your letter? Oh, yes. I did see it but I didn't open it. My mind was on Sibyl. Oh and I read some of that book you sent me. It fascinated me so much. While I was waiting for Sibyl, I almost forgot the time. Oh, I'd rather you weren't here when she arrives.

LORD HENRY: Yes. I thought you'd like it.

DORIAN: I didn't say I liked it, Harry. I said it fascinated me. There's a great difference.

LORD HENRY: Oh. You have discovered that?

DORIAN: You think you can cut life to pieces with a few glib epigrams.

LORD HENRY: You know nothing then?

DORIAN: Nothing?

LORD HENRY: Dorian, my, my letter—don't be afraid. Was to tell you that Sibyl Vane is dead . . .

DORIAN: That's the most horrible lie you have ever perpetrated—even to me! How dare you!

LORD HENRY: I'm sorry, Dorian, but I'm afraid it's quite true. It's in all the morning papers. I thought you would have seen them by now, which is why I wrote and asked you not to see anyone until I came round. There will be an inquest, of course, but naturally you must not be mixed up with it. If anyone should have heard your name at the theatre, like the

girl's mother, I'm sure it can all be arranged. These things
always can be. In Paris it might make a man seem
fashionable but in London people are so prejudiced. Here,
one should never make one's début with a scandal. One
should reserve that to give an interest to one's old age. I'm
sure nobody recognized any of us in that little place.

DORIAN: Recognized? Inquest? What do you mean by it? Do you
mean that Sibyl——? Tell me—the whole thing.

LORD HENRY: I don't think there's any question of it being an
accident, Dorian. Though it could be put that way to the
public, and as we know, they can be made to believe
anything. I won't go into details, you can read those for
yourself, but it seems that she was found dead on her
dressing-room floor. According to the papers, they seemed
to think she'd swallowed something by mistake, something
they use in theatres for some reason. I don't know what it
was but it had either prussic acid or white lead in it. I
should fancy it was prussic acid. She seems to have died
instantaneously . . .

DORIAN: That is something, but not very much, all the same.

LORD HENRY: Yes. It's very tragic. But you must not allow yourself to get mixed up in it. I see in *The Standard* that she
was seventeen. I'd have thought she was even younger than
that. She looked such a child . . . Dorian, you are not to let
this thing bring you down. I will tell you what you will do.
This evening you will come and dine with me and afterwards
we will look in at the Opera. Yes, the Opera. It is a Patti
night and everybody will be there. You can come to my
sister's box. She'll have some smart women with her . . .

DORIAN: So: I have murdered Sibyl Vane. Just as if I'd cut her
throat myself with a knife.

(*He looks out into the garden.*)

The sun shines and the birds sing. And tonight, I'm going
to dine with you, then go on to the Opera, and sup
somewhere afterwards. How extraordinarily theatrical this
would have seemed if one had watched it happen . . .
Somehow, now that it has happened actually, and to me, it's
too much to contemplate at one time. That was the first real

love letter I've ever written in my life. The first and that to a girl already dead. Do you think they can feel? Sibyl? Do you think she can feel or know or listen? And then did I really love her? Last night she tried to explain herself to me. But I wasn't moved one bit. She just seemed shallow to me. Then afterwards, something made me feel afraid. I don't know what it was but it was horrible. I knew I'd done wrong, that I'd have to go back to her. Well, there she is—dead. My God! Harry, what shall I do? I don't think you know the danger I'm in. And there's nothing to keep me straight. Perhaps she could have done that for me. She'd no right to kill herself. No *right*.

(LORD HENRY *begins to relax and takes out a cigarette from his case.*)

LORD HENRY: My dear Dorian, the only way a woman can ever reform a man is by boring him so completely that he loses all possible interest in life. If you had married this girl, you would have been wretched. Of course, you would have treated her kindly. One can always be kind to people about whom one cares nothing, but she would have soon found out that you were absolutely indifferent to her. And when a woman finds that out about her husband—well, I assure you that in any case the whole thing would have been an absolute failure.

DORIAN: I suppose it would. I remember your saying once that there is a fatality about good resolutions—that they are always made too late.

LORD HENRY: There is always some luxury to be had in self-reproach.

DORIAN: Harry, why is it that I can't feel all of this as much as I want to? I know that I'm not heartless. Do you think I am?

LORD HENRY: You have done too many foolish things during the last fortnight to be entitled to give yourself that crown.

DORIAN: I don't like that explanation but I am glad at least you don't think I'm heartless. I am nothing like that. I know I'm not. But still I know, and I'm telling you this, that what has just happened isn't affecting me as it should. It only seems like the perfect ending to a perfect play. Like a

Greek tragedy in which I'd have taken part but not been wounded at all.

LORD HENRY: You know, it does often happen that life's real tragedies take place in such an unartistic manner that they only hurt us by their crude violence. By their absolute incoherence, their absurd want of meaning, to say nothing of their entire lack of style. They affect us just as vulgarity affects us. They give us an impression of sheer brute force. And what is sensitive within us revolts against that very thing. On the other hand, sometimes a tragedy that holds true artistic beauty crosses our lives. If those elements are real, then the whole thing simply appeals to our sense of dramatic effect. Suddenly we find that we are no longer the actors but the spectators of the play. Or rather we are both. We watch ourselves and the mere wonder of the spectacle enthralls us. In this particular case, what is it that has *really* happened? Someone has killed herself for love of you. I wish such a thing had ever happened to me. It would have made me in love with love for the rest of my life. The people who have adored me—there have not been very many but there have been some—have always insisted on going on long after I have ceased to care for them or they to care for me. The one charm of the past is that it is the past. But women never know when the curtain has fallen. They always want a very last act and as soon as the interest of the play is entirely over, they want to go on continuing it. If they were allowed their own way, every comedy would have a tragic ending and every tragedy would culminate in farce. They are full of artifice but they have no sense of art. You are much more fortunate than I am. I assure you, Dorian, that not one of the women I have known would have done for me what Sibyl Vane has done for you. Ordinary women always console themselves. Yes, there is really no end to the consolations that women find in modern life. Really, Dorian, how different Sibyl must have been from all the women one meets! There is something almost beautiful about her death. And I am glad, yes glad, to be living in a century when such wonders can still *happen*. They make one believe in the reality of the things we all play with.

DORIAN: Such as?

LORD HENRY: Oh, romance, passion, love.

DORIAN: I was inhumanly cruel to her. You seem to forget that.

LORD HENRY: I am afraid that women appreciate cruelty, downright cruelty, more than anything else. They have wonderfully primitive instincts. You may emancipate them but they remain slaves looking for their masters, all the same.

DORIAN: I don't know what you're talking about—all I know is that she'll never come to life again now.

LORD HENRY: No, she will never come to life. She has played her last part. But you must think of that lonely death in some tatty dressing-room as something else. The girl never really lived. And so she has never really died.

(*After a darkening silence,* DORIAN *looks up.*)

DORIAN: Well, Harry, you seem to have explained myself to me. I wonder if you know me as well as you seem to think. I don't want us to talk about this again. Ever. It has been an experience. That is all. I can't think that there can be much else in store.

LORD HENRY: Life has everything in store for you, Dorian. There is nothing that you, with everything you have, won't be able to do.

DORIAN: But what if I—change?

LORD HENRY: Ah, then, then, my dear Dorian, you will have to fight your own victories. As it is, they are brought to you. No, you must keep what you have, and what you appear to be. We live in an age that reads too much to be wise and that thinks too much to be beautiful. We cannot spare you. And now you'd better dress and drive down to the Club. We are rather late as it is.

DORIAN: I think I shall join you at the Opera. I feel too tired to eat anything. What is the number of your sister's box?

LORD HENRY: Twenty-seven, I believe. It is on the Grand Tier. You will see her name on the door. But I'm sorry you won't come and dine.

DORIAN: I don't feel up to it. But I'm awfully obliged to you for everything.

LORD HENRY: We are only at the beginning of our friendship, Dorian. Good-bye. I shall see you before nine-thirty, I hope. Remember, Patti is singing.

(*He goes out. As he closes the door behind him,* DORIAN *touches the bell and presently* VICTOR *appears.*)

VICTOR: You rang, *monsieur*?

DORIAN: I shall be going to the Opera this evening.

VICTOR: Very well, *monsieur*. I shall put out your clothes.

DORIAN: Oh, later will do. In the meantime, I want you to go round to Mr. Hubbard. He is the frame-maker in South Audley Street. I have some pictures I want his advice about.

VICTOR: I know the gentleman, *monsieur*.

DORIAN (*impatiently*): Tell him it's most important and I should like him to come round as soon as possible. That's all. Oh, and ask Mrs. Leaf to give you the key of the schoolroom.

VICTOR: The old schoolroom, *monsieur*? It's so long that anyone has gone into it it must be full of dust. I'll see to it that she puts it straight before you go into it. I'm sure it's not fit for you to look at, *monsieur*.

DORIAN: I don't want it put straight, Victor, by you or Mrs. Leaf or anyone. I only want the key. Do you understand that?

VICTOR: Just as you wish, *monsieur*. I thought you might be covered with cobwebs if you went into it. Mrs. Leaf tells me that it hasn't been opened for nearly five years, not since his Lordship died.

DORIAN: That is unimportant. I simply want to see the place, that's all.

VICTOR: Yes, *monsieur*. Mr. Hallward is waiting to see you. Shall I send him in?

DORIAN: Yes. And then get off to the frame-maker's.

(DORIAN *watches* VICTOR *go out and then hurriedly makes sure that the screen over the portrait is intact. He picks up a newspaper and glances at it before going over to the window and looking out. Enter* BASIL HALLWARD.)

BASIL: My dear Dorian, I'm so glad to find you in. I saw Harry in the street on my way here. He seemed almost bland about this whole horrible business. It must be awful for you. I thought you might be with the police or something.

DORIAN: Why should I be with the police?

BASIL: Oh, Harry said something about you actually going to the Opera tonight. I couldn't believe it. I do hope you won't get too involved.

DORIAN: Involved? Why should I be involved?

BASIL: Surely you must know that better than I.

DORIAN: As a matter of fact I *am* going to the Opera.

BASIL: Going? To the Opera?

DORIAN: Yes, why don't you come? I am meeting Lady Gwendolen, Harry's sister, for the first time. We are all meeting in her box.

BASIL: That's what Harry told me. Also, of course, that she is perfectly charming and that Patti will sing divinely.

DORIAN: Don't talk about horrid subjects, Basil. One can go on talking about something as if nothing else had ever happened. So often it's merely the expression that appears to give reality to things. And in these days, as you must know, it is increasingly hard to know what is real or not. Whether a love affair has ended or a child is dead.

BASIL: Dorian, Sibyl Vane has been lying dead in some lodging house or wherever it may be—and people talk about other women being charming and of Patti singing divinely! Why, the girl you loved hasn't even yet found a grave to crawl into for all we know. Let alone whatever else may face her then!

DORIAN: Don't go on to me, Basil! You must not tell me about things . . . What is past is past.

BASIL: You call yesterday the past?

DORIAN: All I know is that I don't want to be at the mercy of my emotions. I want to use them, to enjoy them. And to dominate them.

BASIL: But that's horrible. Something has changed you. To me you look the same creature who, day after day, used to come down to my studio to sit for his picture. But you were simple, natural and affectionate then. You were the most unspoilt character in the whole world. Now, I don't know what's come over you. You talk as if you had no heart, no pity in you. Is it Harry's influence?

DORIAN: I owe a great deal to him, Basil. More than I owe to you. You only taught me to be vain.

BASIL: Well, I am punished for that, Dorian—or shall be some day.

DORIAN: I don't know what you mean or what you want. What *do* you want?

BASIL: I want the Dorian Gray I used to paint.

DORIAN: When I heard that Sibyl Vane had killed herself——

BASIL: Killed herself! You mean there isn't any doubt about it?

DORIAN: Surely you don't think it was a vulgar accident? Of course she killed herself.

BASIL: How awful.

DORIAN: No, there is nothing awful about it. It is one of the great romantic tragedies of the age. As a rule, people who act lead the most commonplace lives. They are good husbands, or faithful wives, or something tedious. You know what I mean—middle-class virtue, and all that kind of thing. How different Sibyl was to that! She *lived* her finest tragedy. She was always a heroine. The last night she played—the night you saw her—she acted badly because she'd known the reality of love. When she knew its unreality, she died, as Juliet might have died. She passed again into the sphere of art. Her death has all the pathetic uselessness of martyrdom, all its wasted beauty. But, as I was saying, you must not think I have not suffered. If you had come in earlier—a particular moment—about half-past five, perhaps, or a quarter to six— you might have found me in tears. Even Harry, who was here, who brought me the news, in fact, had no idea what I was going through. I suffered immensely. Then it passed away. I cannot repeat an emotion. No one can, except sentimentalists. And you are awfully unjust, Basil. You come down here to console me. You *find* me consoled, and you are furious. How like a sympathetic person! You remind me of a story Harry told me about a certain philanthropist who spent twenty years of his life in trying to get some grievance redressed, or some unjust law altered—I forget exactly what it was. Finally he succeeded, and nothing could exceed his disappointment. He had absolutely nothing to do, almost died of *ennui*, and became a confirmed misanthrope. I love beautiful things that one can touch and handle. But the artistic temperament that they create, or at any rate reveal, is still more to me. To become the spectator of one's own life, as Harry says, is to escape the suffering of life. I know you are surprised at my talking to you like this. You have not realized how I have developed. I was a schoolboy when you knew me. I have new passions, new thoughts, new ideas. I am different, but you must not like me less. I am changed, but you must always be my friend. Of course I am very fond of Harry. But I know that you are better than he is. You are not stronger—you are too much afraid of life—but you are better. And how happy we used to be together! Don't leave me, Basil, and don't quarrel with me. I am what I am. There is nothing more to be said.

BASIL: Well, Dorian, I won't speak to you again about this horrible thing, after today. I only trust your name won't be mentioned in connection with it. The inquest is to take place this afternoon. Have they summoned you?

(DORIAN *shakes his head and a look of annoyance passes over his face at the mention of the word 'inquest'*.)

DORIAN: You must do me a drawing of Sibyl, Basil. I should like to have something more of her than the memory of a few kisses and a few words.

BASIL: I will try and do something, Dorian, if it would please you. But you must come and sit to me yourself again. I can't get on without you.

DORIAN: I can never sit to you again, Basil. It is impossible!

BASIL: My dear boy, what nonsense! Do you mean to say you don't like what I did of you? Where is it? Why have you pulled the screen in front of it? Let me look at it. It is the best thing I have ever done. Do take the screen away, Dorian. It is simply disgraceful of your servant hiding my work like that. I *felt* the room looked different as I came in.

DORIAN: My servant has nothing to do with it, Basil. You don't imagine I let him arrange my room for me? No; I did it myself. The light was too strong on the portait.

BASIL: Too strong! Surely not, my dear fellow? It is an admirable place for it. Let me see it.

(BASIL *walks towards the corner of the room.*)

DORIAN: Basil, you must not look at it. I don't wish you to.

BASIL: Not look at my own work! You are not serious? Why shouldn't I look at it?

DORIAN: If you try to look at it, Basil, on my word of honour I will never speak to you again as long as I live. I am quite serious. I don't offer any explanation, and you are not to ask for any. But, remember, if you touch this screen, everything is over between us.

BASIL: Dorian!

DORIAN: Don't speak!

BASIL: But what is the matter? Of course I won't look at it if you don't want me to. But, really, it seems rather absurd that I shouldn't see my own work, especially as I am going to exhibit it in Paris in the autumn. I shall probably have to give it another coat of varnish before that, so I must see it some day, and why not today?

DORIAN: You want to exhibit it?

BASIL: Yes; I don't suppose you will object to that. Georges Petit is going to collect all my best pictures for a special exhibition in the Rue de Sèze, which will open the first week in October. The portrait will only be away a month. I should think you could easily spare it for that time. And if you keep it always behind a screen, you can't care much about it.

DORIAN: You told me a month ago that you would never exhibit it. Why have you changed your mind? You people who go in for being consistent have just as many moods as others have. The only difference is that your moods are rather meaningless. You can't have forgotten that you assured me most solemnly that nothing in the world would induce you to send it to any exhibition. You told Harry exactly the same thing. Basil, we have each of us a secret. Let me know yours and I shall tell you mine. What was your reason for refusing to exhibit my picture?

BASIL: Dorian, if I told you, you might like me less than you do, and you would certainly laugh at me. I could not bear your doing either of those two things. If you wish me never to look at your picture again, I am content. I have always you to look at. If you wish the best work I have ever done to be hidden from the world, I am satisfied. Your friendship is dearer to me than any fame or reputation.

DORIAN: No, Basil, you must tell me. I think I have a right to know.

BASIL: Let us sit down, Dorian. Let us sit down. And just answer me one question. Have you noticed in the picture something curious? Something that probably at first didn't strike you, but that suddenly . . . revealed itself to you? I see you did. Don't speak. Wait till you hear what I have to say. Dorian, from the moment I met you, your personality had the most extraordinary influence over me. I was dominated, soul, brain, and power by you. You became to me the visible incarnation of that unseen ideal . . . Well—I worshipped you. I grew jealous of everyone you spoke to. I wanted to have you all to myself. I was only happy when I was with you. When you were away from me you were still present in my art . . . Of course I never let you know anything about this. It would have been impossible. You would not have understood. I hardly understood it myself. I only knew that I had seen perfection face to face, and that the world had become wonderful to my eyes—too wonderful, perhaps, for in such worship there is peril . . . Weeks and weeks went on, and I grew more and more absorbed. Whether it was the realism of the method, or wonder of your own personality I can't tell. But I know that as I worked at it, every flake and film of colour seemed to me to reveal my secret. I felt, Dorian, that I had told too much, that I had put too much of myself into it. Then it was that I resolved never to allow the picture to be exhibited. You were a little annoyed; but then you didn't realize all that it meant to me. Harry laughed at me about it but I didn't mind that. When the picture was finished, and I sat alone with it, I felt that I was right . . . Well, after a few days the thing left my studio, and as soon as I had got rid of it, it seemed to me that I had been foolish in imagining that I had seen anything more in it. Even now I cannot help feeling that it is a mistake to think that the passion one feels in creation is ever really shown in the work one creates. Art is always more abstract than we fancy. It often seems to me that art conceals the artist far more completely than it ever reveals him. And so when I got this offer from Paris I determined to make your portrait the principal thing in my exhibition. It never occurred to me that you would refuse. I see now that you were right. The picture cannot be shown. You must *not* be angry with me, Dorian. As I said to Harry, once, you are made for this kind of thing. It is extraordinary to me, Dorian, that you should have seen this in the portrait. Did you really see it?

DORIAN: I saw something in it. Something that seemed very curious.

BASIL: Well, you don't mind my looking at the thing now?

DORIAN: You must not ask me that, Basil.

BASIL: You will some day, surely?

DORIAN: Never.

BASIL: Well, perhaps you are right. And now, good-bye, Dorian. You have been the one person in my life who has really influenced my art. Whatever I have done that is good, I owe to you. Ah! You don't know what it cost me to tell you all that I have told you.

DORIAN: My dear Basil, what have you told me? Simply that you felt that you admired me too much. That is not even a compliment.

BASIL: It was not intended as a compliment. It was a confession. Now that I have made it, something seems to have gone out of me.

DORIAN: It was a very disappointing confession.

BASIL: Why, what did you expect, Dorian? You didn't see anything else in the picture, did you? There was nothing else to see?

DORIAN: No; there was nothing else to see. Why do you ask? You and I are friends, Basil, and we always will be.

BASIL: You have got Harry.

DORIAN: Oh, Harry! Harry spends his days in saying what is incredible, and his evenings in doing what is improbable. Just the sort of life I would like to lead. But still I don't think I would go to Harry if I were in trouble. I'd sooner go to you, Basil.

BASIL: You will sit to me again?

DORIAN: It's impossible!

BASIL: No man came across two ideal things. Few come across *one*.

DORIAN: There is something fatal about a portrait. It has a life of its own. I will come and have tea with you. That will be just as pleasant.

BASIL: Pleasanter for you, I am afraid. And now good-bye again. I am sorry you won't let me look at the picture once again. But that can't be helped. I quite understand what you feel about it.

(*As he makes to go out,* VICTOR *knocks and enters.*)

It's all right. I'll see myself out.

DORIAN: Well?

VICTOR: I have obtained the key to the schoolroom from Mrs. Leaf.

DORIAN: Very well. Leave it on the table. You can go.

(BASIL *goes.*)

VICTOR: Yes, *monsieur*. Only the person from the frame-maker's is here.

DORIAN: Mr. Hubbard?

VICTOR: Yes, *monsieur*.

DORIAN: Ask him to wait a few moments. Oh, I'll call him myself when I wish to see him.

VICTOR: Will there be anything else, *monsieur*?

DORIAN: No. When Mr. Hubbard has gone, you can put out my clothes for the evening. I wish to see him alone. Oh—is there another key existing to the schoolroom?

VICTOR: Mrs. Leaf says she has the only one. She's most anxious to clean it out before——

DORIAN: Yes. That will be all.

(VICTOR *nods and goes out, leaving* DORIAN *watching him. He locks the door behind the servant and then goes to the table and*

*picks up the key to the schoolroom. Then he ascends the
short staircase. He unlocks the door and we see him
enter the room. His back reappears. He is carrying a large,
purple coverlet which catches the light from the open
door of the schoolroom. He comes back into the room and places
the heavy coverlet over the portrait. He then pulls some of
the window curtains, leaving the room in partial, heavy darkness. He pauses, then gives a final look at the portrait itself. He
seems about to reel at what he sees when a knock at the
door stops him.)*

VOICE OFF: Mr. Gray, sir!

DORIAN: Coming, coming!

*(He rearranges the picture as before, unlocks the door and
admits MR. HUBBARD.)*

Please forgive me for keeping you waiting. I was feeling a
little unwell. How kind of you to come so soon.

MR. HUBBARD: Always a pleasure to do anything for you, Mr.
Gray. Always. Drop anything, as they say, to oblige a
gentleman like yourself. My, it's dark in here.

DORIAN: I have rather a severe headache.

MR. HUBBARD: Yes sir, What can I do for you, Mr. Gray. I
thought I'd do myself the honour of coming round in
person. I've just got a beauty of a frame, sir. Picked it up at a
sale. Old Florentine. Came from Fonthill, I believe.
Admirably suited for a religious subject, Mr. Gray.

DORIAN: I am so sorry you have given yourself the trouble of
coming round, Mr. Hubbard. I shall certainly drop in
and look at the frame—though I don't go in much at
present for religious art—but today I only want a picture
carried to the top of the house for me. It is rather heavy, so
I thought I would ask you to lend me a couple of your men.

MR. HUBBARD: No trouble at all, Mr. Gray. I am delighted to be
of any service to you. Which is the work of art, sir?

DORIAN: This. Can you move it, covering and all, just as it is? I
don't want it to get scratched going upstairs.

MR. HUBBARD: There will be no difficulty, sir. Would you and
I——?

DORIAN: Yes. You and I can manage well enough . . .

71

MR. HUBBARD: And, now, where shall we carry it to, Mr. Gray?

DORIAN: I will show you the way, Mr. Hubbard, if you will kindly follow me. Or perhaps you had better go in front. I am afraid it is right up here. We'll go up by the front staircase; it's wider.

(*They pass out on to the staircase and begin the ascent. The elaborate character of the frame makes the picture extremely bulky, and now and then, in spite of the obsequious protests of* MR. HUBBARD, DORIAN *puts his hands to it so as to help more.*)

MR. HUBBARD: Something of a load to carry, sir.

(*They reach the top landing and* MR. HUBBARD *wipes his shiny forehead.*)

DORIAN: I am afraid it *is* rather heavy.

(*He opens wide the door of the schoolroom. They are now silhouettes in the room.*)

DORIAN: Oh, anywhere. Here: this will do. I don't want to have it hung. Just lean it against the wall. Thanks.

MR. HUBBARD: Might one look at the work of art, sir?

DORIAN: It would not interest you, Mr. Hubbard. I shan't trouble you any more now. I am much obliged for your kindness in coming round.

MR. HUBBARD: Not at all, not at all, Mr. Gray. Ever ready to do anything for you, sir.

(MR. HUBBARD *tramps downstairs, followed by* DORIAN. DORIAN *shows* HUBBARD *out. He locks the door and wipes his brow. His eye lights on the newspaper.*)

DORIAN (*reading*): 'Inquest on an Actress.'

(*He tears it up and draws the curtain. Sits.*)

Act Three

SCENE I

*Dorian's rooms. They are in semi-darkness but there is a fire of
indolent activity about them. It is full of figures, earlier characters
from the story:* SIBYL, *her* BROTHER, BASIL, LORD HENRY, AUNT
AGATHA *and so on. They are recognizable but grotesque. Mauling,
groaning, shrieking, giggling in the strange light. After some time,
there is the sound of a hansom drawing up. Immediately* DORIAN *enters
it is clear—the difference between him and these creatures. He is
beautifully dressed in evening clothes but the difference is immediate on
his entrance. In face and figure, he has remained exactly the same. The
figures in the room are all twenty-year travesties of what they were.
Only he has retained the exact outward form. He comes into the room
and takes in the spectacle perfunctorily. Then, without even taking off
his hat and leaving his cane, he rushes up to the schoolroom. When he
has unlocked this, surveyed it and re-locked it, he stands at the top of
the stairs and speaks.*

During this speech, he addresses severally SIBYL, JAMES, LORD
HENRY, *everyone in fact, including the auditorium.*

DORIAN: Mysticism. How fairly easy it is to take up its common
power? And what is that power? Simply that of making
common things seem strange—to us . . . I know these people
—or they think they have known me, I have been more—
more *curious*. That, at least, I have taught myself to be. And
yet, I've not been really reckless. Once or twice during the
month, and on each Wednesday evening while the season
has lasted, I've thrown open my house to what, to those,
who are considered to be, among the very best. And given,
what even they have acknowledged to be, the very best.
Which is why they come. And, also, sometimes, even to see
me. Or gaze at me in my own surroundings . . . The

73

worship of the senses has often—and with much justice—
been decried. Men—and, of course—of course?—women?
Anyway, a lot do have a natural instinct of terror about
passions and sensations seeming stranger than themselves.
But it's always seemed to me, at any rate, that such things
can't be *killed*. A resistance sets in. Loss! So much sur-
rendered. By me and those before me. Wilful rejections,
self-torture and denial and God knows what! But I believe,
and I do believe this, whatever may be its opposite
happening, that there will be a new life, a new kind, kind—
sort, way, access to life, to re-create it. We may yet save
ourselves from the uncomely puritanism that revives itself
in our own day. Now. As I speak. Out of time. History.
Past. Present. Me. Experience itself. But not its fruits.
There can't be many of us who've not woken up before
dawn. Dreamless nights better than any death. When
everything, all is, disorder . . . Terror. Flashing in the
darkness. Figures. Faces. Half faces. There they are. There
they've gone. Shadows, flickers, unreal, oh, God, where is
the real life we might have known! Could we know it. And
yet we have to resume, resume, as if it took no place or had
never mattered. There is this necessity for, necessity, a
continuance of energy, energy in the same wearisome round
of stereotyped habits. Open my eyelids to a re-world! I
tried to create, not create, model, re-model a world. World
of what? Objects? Perfume? Scent? Musk that troubles the
brain troubled already. Champak that stains the imagination,
the world of smell, of root, pollen, balms and aroma; dark,
fragrant woods; spikenard, hovenia that makes men mad and
aloes that are said, said, to be able to drive out melancholy
from the man . . . And music? The strangest instruments
to be found, either in tombs of dead nations or savage ones
that have to survive and touch? Earthen pans of Peruvians
with the shrill cries of birds and flutes of human bones.
Aztec bells hung in clusters like grapes; vibrating tongues of
wood. And so to Wagner . . . Jewels? Days spent with
collections, yes, collections—the cymophane with its wine-
like line of silver, the pistachio-coloured peridot, rose-pink

74

and wine-yellow topazes, carbuncles of fiery scarlet with
tremulous four-rayed stars, flame-red cinnamon stones,
orange and violet spinels, amethysts with alternate layers of
ruby and sapphire. Red gold of sunstone, moonstone and
milky opal. Stones: Henry VIII on his way to the Tower with
a jacket of raised gold, the placard embroidered with
diamonds and a great bauderike about his neck of large
balasses. Elizabeth, James, the Duke of Burgundy . . .
Embroidery and the chill rooms of Northern Europe.
Time . . . What it has all once been . . . I can't be out of
England long . . . For all that . . . Portrait or no. Who
believes such things. Do I? Is insincerity such a terrible thing.
I think not. It's merely a method by which we can multiply
our personalities. Like all of you! Get out of here. Except
you, Basil. You stay a little, Basil. How old you seem.
(*They all disappear except for* BASIL, *who is dressed for
travelling.*)
What a way for a fashionable painter to travel. A Gladstone
bag and an ulster. Just mind you don't talk about anything
serious. Nothing is serious nowadays. At least, nothing
should be. What is it all about? I hope it is not about
myself. I am tired of myself tonight. I should like to be
somebody else.

BASIL: It *is* about yourself. I think it right that you should know
that the most dreadful things are being said against
you in London.

DORIAN: I don't wish to know anything about them. I love
scandals about other people, but scandals about myself don't
interest me.

BASIL: Oh, that's Harry. They must interest you, Dorian. Every
gentleman is interested in his good name. You don't want
people to talk of you as something vile and degraded. Of
course you have your position, and your wealth, and all that
kind of thing. But position and wealth are not everything.
Mind you, I don't believe these rumours at all. At least, I
can't believe them when I see you. Sin is a thing that writes
itself across a man's face. It can't be concealed. People talk
sometimes of secret vices. There are no such things. If a

wretched man has a vice, it shows itself in the lines of his mouth, the droop of his eyelids, the moulding of his hands even. Somebody—I won't mention his name, but you know him—came to me last year to have his portrait done. I had never heard anything about him at the time, though I have heard a good deal since. His life is dreadful. But you, Dorian, with your pure, bright innocent face, and your marvellous untroubled youth—I can't believe anything against you. And yet I see you very seldom, and you never come down to the studio now, and when I am away from you, and I hear all these hideous things that people are whispering about you, I don't know what to say. Why is it, Dorian, that a man like the Duke of Berwick leaves the room of a club when you enter it? Why is it that so many gentlemen in London will neither go to your house nor invite you to theirs? You used to be a friend of Lord Staveley. I met him at dinner last week. Staveley just said that you might have the most artistic tastes, but that you were a man whom no pure-minded girl should be allowed to know, and whom no chaste woman should sit in the same room with. I reminded him that I was a friend of yours, and asked him what he meant. He told me. He told me right out in front of everybody. It was horrible! Why is your friendship so fatal? What about Adrian Singleton, and his end?

DORIAN: Stop, Basil. You are talking about things you know nothing about. You ask me why Berwick leaves a room when I enter it. It is because I know everything about his life, not because he knows anything about mine. With such blood as he has in his veins, how could his record be clean? If Kent's silly son takes his wife from the streets, what is that to me? If Adrian Singleton writes his friend's name across a bill, am I his keeper? I know how people chatter in England. The middle classes air their moral prejudices over their gross dinner-tables, and whisper about what they call the profligacies of their betters in order to try and pretend that they are in smart society, and on intimate terms with the people they slander. In this country it is enough for a man to have distinction and brains for every common tongue to wag against him. And what sort of lives do these people, who pose as being moral, lead themselves? My dear fellow, you forget that we are in the native land of the hypocrite.

BASIL: Dorian, that is not the question. England is bad enough, I know, and English society is all wrong. That is the reason why I want you to be fine. You have not been fine. One has a right to judge of a man by the effect he has over his friends. I know you and Harry are inseparable. Surely for that reason, if for none other, you should not have made his sister's name a byword.

DORIAN: Take care, Basil. You go too far.

BASIL: I must speak, and you must listen. You shall listen. When you met Lady Gwendolen, not a breath of scandal had ever touched her. Is there a single decent woman in London now who would drive with her in the Park? Why, even her children are not allowed to live with her. Then there are other stories—Don't shrug your shoulders like that. Don't be so indifferent. You have a wonderful influence. Let it be for good, not for evil. They say that you corrupt everyone with whom you become intimate, and that it is quite sufficient for you to enter a house, for shame of some kind to follow after. I don't know whether it is so or not. How should I know? Know you? I wonder: do I know you? Before I could answer that, I should have to see your soul.

DORIAN: To see my soul!

BASIL: Yes. But only God can do that.

DORIAN: You shall see it yourself, tonight!

(*As he says this, he seizes a lamp from the table.*)

Come: it is your own handiwork. Why shouldn't you look at it? You can tell the world all about it afterwards, if you choose. Nobody would believe you. If they did believe you, they would like me all the better for it. I know the age better than you do, though you will prate about it so tediously. Come, I tell you. You have chattered enough about corruption. Now you shall look on it face to face.

BASIL: You must not say things like that. They don't mean anything.

DORIAN: You think so?

77

BASIL: I know so. As for what I said to you tonight, I said it for your good. You know I have been always a staunch friend to you.

DORIAN: Finish what you have to say . . . I am waiting, Basil.

BASIL: What I have to say is this. You must give me some answer . . .

DORIAN: Come upstairs, Basil. I keep a diary of my life from day to day, and it never leaves the room in which it is written. I shall show it to you if you come with me.

BASIL: I shall come with you, Dorian, if you wish it. I see I have missed my train. That makes no matter. I can go tomorrow. But don't ask me to read anything tonight. All I want is a plain answer to my question.

DORIAN: That shall be given to you upstairs. I could not give it here. You will not have to read long.

(They go up the stairs to the schoolroom.)

It is my birthday. Tomorrow. You shall have lost your train.

(They reach the top. DORIAN sets the lamp down on the floor, takes out the key and turns it in the lock.)

You insist on knowing?

BASIL: Yes. Now.

DORIAN: I'm delighted. You are entitled to know whatever there is to know. After all, our lives have mingled as much as most in these days.

(He opens the door of the schoolroom and sets the lamp down. They hover within the room as BASIL stares around him, then at the portrait with its screen over it.)

You still think only God sees such things? Draw back the curtain . . .

BASIL: You're mad, Dorian. Or playing a part.

DORIAN: You won't? Then I shall. It's too late for prayer, Basil, if that's what you're thinking of.

(He tears away the screen. The lamp falls. BASIL screams. Then gets to his knees.)

BASIL: Dorian. Kneel, Dorian. Kneel with me. If you can.

DORIAN: I told you, Basil. Prayer comes too late.

BASIL: Kneel with me, Dorian. Kneel.

78

DORIAN: Very well.

(*We see him take a knife from within the room. He closes the door and we see the silhouettes of the two men kneeling. Then another scream and a body falls. Silence. After a while, the following happens: the door opens.* BASIL *is lying inert on the floor.* DORIAN *remembers the lamp in the room, returns for it, seats* BASIL'S *body at the table, locks the door, leaving the room in darkness.*

Having locked the door behind him, he creeps downstairs. The woodwork creaks. He stops and listens. But he is alone. When he descends, he sees Basil's bag and coat. He unlocks a secret press in the wainscoting. Inside are all kinds of strange clothing, things that look like disguises or things rescued from an attic for a particular purpose. He shoves Basil's things in among them, locks the cupboard. Then takes out his watch to look at the time. A sudden thought seems to strike him. He puts on his fur coat and hat, and goes out into the hall. There he pauses, hearing the slow heavy tread of the policeman on the pavement outside, and seeing the flash of the bull's-eye reflected in the window, waits, and holds his breath. After a few moments he draws back the latch, then slips out, shutting the door very gently behind him. Then he begins ringing the bell. His valet appears half-dressed, and looking very drowsy.)

DORIAN: I am sorry to have had to wake you up, Francis, but I had fogotten my latchkey. What times is it?

(*As he says this, he steps in.*)

FRANCIS: Ten minutes past two, sir.

DORIAN: Ten minutes past two? How horribly late! You must wake me at nine tomorrow. I've some work to do.

FRANCIS: All right, sir.

DORIAN: Did anyone call this evening?

FRANCIS: Mr. Hallward, sir. He stayed here till eleven, and then I should think he went away to catch his train.

DORIAN: Oh! I am sorry I didn't see him. Did he leave any message?

FRANCIS: No, sir, except that he would write to you from Paris, if he did not find you at the Club.

DORIAN: That will do, Francis. Don't forget to call me at nine

79

tomorrow.

FRANCIS: No, sir.

(*The man shambles down the passage in his slippers.* DORIAN *throws his hat and coat upon the table and passes into the library. As he does so, he calls out again to* FRANCIS.)

DORIAN: Oh yes, Francis. Tomorrow: tomorrow I shall want to see Alan Campbell, of 152 Hertford Street, Mayfair. If he is out of town, I want his address. You understand?

FRANCIS: Very good, Mr. Gray.

FADE

SCENE II

DORIAN *sits alone in his rooms. Even for him, it is clear he has not slept at all and is unlike his usual bandbox self. The servant enters.*

FRANCIS: Mr. Campbell, sir.

DORIAN: Ask him to come in at once, Francis.

(FRANCIS *bows and goes out and then returns with* ALAN CAMPBELL.)

FRANCIS: Mr. Campbell, sir.

(ALAN CAMPBELL *walks in, looking very stern and rather pale, his pallor being intensified by his coal-black hair and dark eyebrows.*)

DORIAN: Alan! This is kind of you! I thank you for coming.

ALAN: I had intended never to enter your house again, Gray. But you said it was a matter of life and death.

DORIAN: Yes: it is a matter of life and death, Alan, and to more than one person. Sit down.

(ALAN *takes a chair by the table, and* DORIAN *sits opposite him. The two men's eyes meet. After a strained moment of silence,* DORIAN *leans across.*)

Alan, in a locked room at the top of this house, a room to which nobody but myself has access, a dead man is seated at a table. He has been dead ten hours now. Don't stir, and don't look at me like that. Who the man is, why he died, how he died, are matters that do not concern you.

80

What you have to do is this——

ALAN: Stop, Gray. I don't want to know anything more. Whether what you have told me is true or not true, doesn't concern me. I entirely decline to be mixed up in your life. Keep your horrible secrets to yourself. They don't interest me any more.

DORIAN: Alan, they will have to interest you. This one will have to interest you. I am awfully sorry for you, Alan. But I can't help myself. You are the one man who is able to save me. I am forced to bring you into the matter. I have no option, Alan, you are scientific. You know about chemistry, and things of that kind. You have made experiments. What you have got to do is to destroy the thing that is upstairs—to destroy it so that not a vestige of it will be left. Nobody saw this person come into the house. Indeed, at the present moment he is supposed to be in Paris. He will not be missed for months. When he is missed, there must be no trace of him found here. You, Alan, you must change him, and everything that belongs to him, into a handful of ashes that I may scatter in the air.

ALAN: You are mad, Dorian.

DORIAN: Ah! I was waiting for you to call me Dorian.

ALAN: You are mad, I tell you—mad to imagine that I would raise a finger to help you, mad to make this monstrous confession. I will have nothing to do with this matter, whatever it is. Do you think I am going to imperil my reputation for you? What is it to me what devil's work you are up to?

DORIAN: It was suicide, Alan.

ALAN: I'm glad to hear it. But who drove him to it? You, I should fancy.

DORIAN: Do you still refuse to do this for me?

ALAN: Of course I refuse. I will have absolutely nothing to do with it. I don't care what shame comes on you. You deserve it all. I shouldn't be sorry to see you disgraced and publicly disgraced. How dare you ask me, of all men in the world, to mix myself up in this! I should have thought you knew more about people's characters. Your friend Lord Henry Wotton can't have taught you much about psychology, whatever else he has taught you. You have come to the wrong man. Go to some of your friends. Don't come to *me*.

DORIAN: Alan, it was murder. I killed him. You don't know what he had made me suffer. Whatever my life is, he had more to do with the making or the marring of it than poor Harry has had. He may not have intended it; the result was the same.

ALAN: Murder! Good God, Dorian, is that what you have come to? I shall not inform upon you. It's not my business. Besides, without my even stirring in the matter, you are certain to be arrested. Nobody ever commits a crime without doing something stupid. But I'll have nothing to do with it.

DORIAN: You must have something to do with it. Wait, wait a moment; listen to me. Only listen, Alan. All I ask of you is to perform a certain scientific experiment. You go to hospitals and dead-houses, and the horrors that you do there don't affect you. If in some hideous dissecting-room, or fetid laboratory you found this man lying on a leaden table with red gutters scooped out in it for the blood to flow through, you'd simply look upon him as an admirable subject. You wouldn't turn a hair. You would not believe that you were doing anything wrong. On the contrary, you would probably feel that you were benefiting the human race, or increasing the aim of knowledge in the world, or gratifying intellectual curiosity, or something of that kind. What I want you to do is merely what you have often done before. And, remember, it is the only piece of evidence against me. If it's discovered, I am lost; and it is sure to be discovered unless you help me.

ALAN: I have no desire to help you. I am simply indifferent to the whole thing. It has nothing to do with me.

DORIAN: Alan, I entreat you. Think of the position I am in. You may know terror yourself some day. Don't inquire now. I have told you too much as it is. But I beg of you to do this. We were friends once, Alan.

ALAN: Don't speak about those days, Dorian: they are dead.

DORIAN: The dead linger sometimes. The man upstairs won't go away. He is sitting at the table with a bowed head and outstretched arms. Alan! If you don't come to my assistance I am ruined. They will hang me for what I have done.

ALAN: I absolutely refuse to do anything. It is insane of you to ask me.

DORIAN: You refuse?

ALAN: Yes.

DORIAN: I entreat you, Alan.

ALAN: It's useless.

(DORIAN *stretches out his hand, takes a piece of paper, and writes something on it. He reads it over twice, folds it carefully, and pushes it across the table. Having done this, he gets up, and goes over to the window.* ALAN *looks at him in surprise, and then takes up the paper, and opens it. After two or three moments' silence,* DORIAN *turns round, and puts his hand upon* ALAN'S *shoulder.*)

DORIAN: I am so sorry for you, Alan, but you leave me no alternative. I have a letter written already. Here it is. You see the address. If you don't help me, I must send it. If you don't help me, I *will* send it. You know what the result will be. But you are going to help me. It is impossible for you to refuse now. I tried to spare you. You will do me the justice to admit that. You treated me as no man has ever dared to treat me—no living man, at any rate. Now it is for me to dictate terms.

(ALAN *buries his face in his hands, and a shudder passes through him.*)

It is my turn to dictate terms, Alan. You know what they are. The thing is quite simple. Come, don't work yourself into a fever. The thing has to be done. Face it, and do it. Come, Alan, you must decide at once.

ALAN: I cannot do it.

DORIAN: You have no choice.

ALAN: Is there a fire in the room upstairs?

DORIAN: Yes, there is a gas-fire with asbestos.

ALAN: I shall have to go home and get some things from the laboratory.

DORIAN: No, Alan, you must *not* leave the house. Write out on a sheet of note-paper what you want, and my servant will take a cab and bring the things back to you.

(ALAN *scrawls a few lines, blots them, and addresses an envelope.* DORIAN *takes the note up and reads it carefully. Then he rings the bell, and gives it to his valet.*)

At once.

(FRANCIS *goes out.*)

ALAN: You are infamous, absolutely infamous!

DORIAN: Hush, Alan: you have saved my life.

ALAN: Your life? What a life *that* is!

DORIAN: Ah, Alan, I wish you had a thousandth part of the pity for me that I have for you.

(ALAN *makes no answer.*)

Now, Alan, there isn't a moment to be lost.

(*He leads him up the stairs. When they reach the top landing,* DORIAN *takes out the key and turns it in the lock. Then he stops.*)

I don't think I can go in, Alan.

ALAN: It is nothing to me. I shan't require you.

(DORIAN *half opens the door. As he does so, he sees the outline of his portrait in the sunlight. On the floor in front of it the torn curtain is lying. He heaves a deep breath, opens the door a little wider, and walks quickly in, determined that he will not look even once upon* BASIL. *Then, stooping down, and taking up the gold and purple hanging, he flings it right over the picture. Then he stops, feeling afraid to turn round, his eyes fixed on the intricacies of the pattern before him.*)

ALAN: Leave me now.

(DORIAN *turns and hurries out. As he does so, Alan's voice follows him.*)

I'll do what you've asked me. And now: let's never see each other again.

DORIAN: You have, *will* have saved me, Alan. I'll not forget that . . .

(*He descends the stairs as* ALAN *closes the door behind him.*)

FADE

84

SCENE III

DORIAN *is still alone. A figure appears.*

DORIAN (*peering*): Is that you, Adrian? Adrian Singleton. I thought you'd left England. Still, I suppose as long as you've got that stuff, you don't want friends, least of all friends; you don't need anything.

(*The figure emerges. It is an older* JAMES VANE.)

JAMES: I'm not Adrian. Adrian! *Or* one of your poor trollop women. Or Sibyl Vane. Remember. Remember her? Sibyl Vane!

(JAMES *struggles with him, to kill him with his bare hands.*)

DORIAN (*croaking*): What do you want? Money!

JAMES: Keep quiet. I'm going to kill you.

DORIAN: You're mad! What have I *done* to you!

JAMES: Sibyl Vane was my sister. She killed herself. I know it. Her death's at your door. I swore I would kill you. I had no clue, no trace. I knew nothing of you but some pet name she used to call you. Make your peace with God, for tonight you are going to *die*.

DORIAN: I never heard of her. You are mad.

JAMES: You had better confess your sin, for as sure as I am James Vane, you are going to die. Down on your knees! I give you one minute to make your peace—no more. I go on board tonight for India, and I must do my job first. One minute. That's all.

(DORIAN's *arms fall to his side.*)

DORIAN (*suddenly*): Stop. How long ago is it since your sister died? Quick, tell me!

JAMES: Eighteen years. Why do you ask me? What do years matter?

DORIAN: Eighteen years! Eighteen years! Set me under the lamp and look at my face!

(JAMES VANE *hesitates for a moment, not understanding. Then he seizes* DORIAN *and drags him into the light. He loosens his hold and reels back.*)

JAMES: My God! My God! And I would have murdered you!

FADE

SCENE IV

DORIAN *is joined by* LORD HENRY *and his cousin, the* DUCHESS OF MONMOUTH—*who is exactly the same actress as* SIBYL VANE. *Merely elevated to the class of the period.*

LORD HENRY: I hope Dorian has told you about my plan for rechristening everything. It is a delightful idea.

DUCHESS OF MONMOUTH: But I don't want to be rechristened, Harry. I am quite satisfied with my own name, and I am sure Mr. Gray should be satisfied with his.

LORD HENRY: It is a sad truth, but we have lost the faculty of giving lovely names to things. Names are everything. I never quarrel with actions. My one quarrel is with words. That is the reason I hate vulgar realism in literature. The man who could call a spade a spade should be compelled to use one. It is the only thing he is fit for.

DUCHESS: Then what should we call you, Harry?

DORIAN: His name is Prince Paradox.

DUCHESS: I recognize him in a flash.

LORD HENRY: I won't hear of it. From a label there is no escape! I refuse the title.

DUCHESS: Royalties may not abdicate.

LORD HENRY: You wish me to defend my throne, then?

DUCHESS: Yes.

LORD HENRY: I give the truths of tomorrow.

DUCHESS: I prefer the mistakes of today.

LORD HENRY: You disarm me. I never tilt against Beauty.

DUCHESS: That is your error, Harry, believe me. You value beauty far too much.

LORD HENRY: How can you say that?

DUCHESS: I admit that I think that it is better to be beautiful than to be good. But on the other hand no one is more ready than I am to acknowledge that it is better to be good than to be ugly.

LORD HENRY: Ugliness is one of the seven deadly virtues. You, as a good Tory, must not underrate them. Beer, the Bible, and the seven deadly virtues have made our England what she is.

DUCHESS: You don't like your country, then?

LORD HENRY: I live in it.

DUCHESS: That you may censure it the better.

LORD HENRY: Would you have me take the verdict of *Europe* on it?

DUCHESS: What do they say of us?

LORD HENRY: That Tartuffe has emigrated to England and opened a shop.

DUCHESS: I believe in the race.

LORD HENRY: It represents the survival of the pushing.

DUCHESS: It has development.

LORD HENRY: Decay fascinates me more.

DUCHESS: What of Art?

LORD HENRY: It is a malady.

DUCHESS: Love?

LORD HENRY: An illusion.

DUCHESS: Religion?

LORD HENRY: The fashionable substitute for Belief.

DUCHESS: You are a sceptic.

LORD HENRY: Never! Scepticism is the beginning of Faith.

DUCHESS: What are you?

LORD HENRY: To define is to limit.

DUCHESS: Give me a clue.

LORD HENRY: Threads snap. You would lose your way in the labyrinth.

DUCHESS: You bewilder me. Let us talk of something else.

LORD HENRY: Our host is a delightful topic.

DORIAN: Ah! Don't remind me of that.

LORD HENRY: Like all good reputations, every effect that one produces gives one an enemy. To be popular one must be a mediocrity.

DUCHESS: Not with women, and women rule the world. I assure you we can't bear mediocrities. We women, as someone says, love with our ears, just as you men love with your eyes, if you ever love at all.

DORIAN: It seems to me that we never do anything else.

DUCHESS: Ah! Then, one never really loves, Mr. Gray? Even when one has been wounded by it?

LORD HENRY: Especially when one has been wounded by it.

DUCHESS: What do you say to that, Mr. Gray?

DORIAN: I always agree with Harry, Duchess.

DUCHESS: Even when he is wrong?

DORIAN: Harry is never wrong, Duchess.

DUCHESS: And does his philosophy make you happy?

DORIAN: I have never searched for happiness. Who wants happiness? I have searched for pleasure.

DUCHESS: And found it, Mr. Gray?

DORIAN: Often. Too often.

DUCHESS: I am searching for peace, and if I don't go and dress, I shall have none this evening.

DORIAN: Let me get you some orchids, Duchess.

(DORIAN *walks down into the conservatory*.)

LORD HENRY: You are flirting disgracefully with him. You had better take care. He is very fascinating.

DUCHESS: If he were not, there would be no battle. Courage has passed from men to women. It is a new experience for us. Describe us as a sex.

LORD HENRY: Sphinxes without secrets.

DUCHESS: How long Mr. Gray is! Let us go and help him. I have not yet told him the colour of my frock.

LORD HENRY: Ah, you must suit your frock to his flowers.

DUCHESS: Women are not always allowed a choice.

(LORD HENRY *sees something is wrong outside with* DORIAN, *who looks about to faint*.)

Is he all right?

LORD HENRY: Yes. Let's leave him a little. (*He turns her back into the room*.) Are you very much in love with him?

DUCHESS: I wish I knew.

LORD HENRY: A mist makes things wonderful.

DUCHESS: One may lose one's way.

LORD HENRY: All ways end at the same point, my dear.

DUCHESS: What is that?

LORD HENRY: Disillusion.

DUCHESS: It was my début in life.

LORD HENRY: It came to you crowned.

DUCHESS: I am tired of strawberry leaves.

LORD HENRY: They become you.

DUCHESS: Only in public.

LORD HENRY: You would miss them.

DUCHESS: I will not part with a petal.

LORD HENRY: Your husband has ears, you know.

DUCHESS: Old age is dull of hearing.

LORD HENRY: Has he never been jealous?

DUCHESS: I wish he had been.

(LORD HENRY *glances about as if in search of something.*)
What are you looking for?

LORD HENRY: The button from your foil. You have dropped it.

DUCHESS: I have still the mask.

LORD HENRY: It makes your eyes lovelier.

(*She laughs and goes out.*)

FADE

SCENE V

DORIAN *and* LORD HENRY *together.* DORIAN's *studio-world.*

LORD HENRY: There is no use your telling me that you are going
to be good. You're quite perfect. Don't change.

DORIAN: No, Harry, I have done too many dreadful things in my
life. I am not going to do any more. I began my good
actions yesterday.

LORD HENRY: Where were you yesterday?

DORIAN: In the country, Harry. I was staying at a little inn by
myself.

LORD HENRY: My dear boy, anybody can be good in the country.
There are no temptations there. That is the reason why
people who live out of town are so absolutely uncivilized.
Civilization is not by any means an easy thing to attain to.
There are only two ways by which man can reach it. One is
by being cultured, the other by being corrupt. Country
people have no opportunity of being either, so they stagnate.

DORIAN: Culture and corruption. I have known something of
both. I am going to alter. I think I *have* altered.

LORD HENRY: You have not yet told me what your good action

89

was. Or did you say you had done more than one?

DORIAN: I can tell you, Harry. It is not a story I could tell to anyone else. I spared somebody. It sounds vain, but you understand what I mean. She was quite beautiful, and wonderfully like Sibyl Vane. I think it was that which first attracted me to her. You remember Sibyl, don't you? How long ago that seems! Well, Hetty was not one of our own class, of course. She was simply a girl in a village. But I really loved her.

LORD HENRY: I thought it was the Duchess who nearly made you faint when you were getting her orchids. Hetty is it?

DORIAN: I am quite sure that I loved her. All during this wonderful May that we have been having, I used to run down and see her two or three times a week. We were to have gone away together this morning at dawn. Suddenly I determined to leave her just as I had found her . . .

LORD HENRY: I should think the novelty of the emotion must have given you a thrill of real pleasure, Dorian. But I can finish your idyll for you. You gave her good advice, and broke her heart. That was the beginning of your reformation.

DORIAN: Harry, you are incorrigible. Hetty's heart is not broken. Of course she cried, and all that. But there is no disgrace on her. She can live.

LORD HENRY: My dear Dorian, you have the most curiously boyish moods. Do you think this girl will ever be really contented now with anyone of her own rank? I suppose she will be married some day to a rough carter or a grinning ploughman. Well, the fact of having met you, and loved you, will teach her to despise her husband, and she will be wretched. From a moral point of view, I cannot say that I think much of your great renunciation. Even as a beginning, it is poor.

DORIAN: Don't let us talk about it any more, and don't try to persuade me that the first good action I have done for years, the first little bit of self-sacrifice I have ever known, is really a sort of sin. I want to be better. I am *going* to be better. Tell me something about yourself. What is going on in town?

LORD HENRY: People are still discussing poor Basil's disappearance.

DORIAN: I should have thought they had got tired of that by this time.

LORD HENRY: My dear boy, they have only been talking about it for six weeks, and the British public are really not equal to the mental strain of having more than one topic every three months. They have been very fortunate lately, however. They have had my own divorce-case, and Alan Campbell's suicide. Now they have got the mysterious disappearance of an artist. Scotland Yard still insists that the man in the grey ulster who left for Paris by the midnight train on the ninth of November was poor Basil, and the French police declare that Basil never arrived in Paris at all. I suppose in about a fortnight we shall be told that he has been seen in San Francisco. It is an odd thing, but everyone who disappears is said to be seen in San Francisco. It must be a delightful city, and possess all the attractions of the next world.

DORIAN: What do you think has happened to Basil?

LORD HENRY: I have not the slightest idea. If Basil chooses to hide himself, it is no business of mine. If he is dead, I don't want to think about him. Death is the only thing that ever terrifies me. I hate it.

DORIAN: Why?

LORD HENRY: Because one can survive everything nowadays except that. Death and vulgarity are the only two facts in the nineteenth century that one cannot explain away.

DORIAN: I was very fond of Basil. Don't people say that he was murdered?

LORD HENRY: Oh, some of the papers do. It does not seem to be at all probable to me. I know there are dreadful places in Paris, but Basil was not the sort of man to have gone to them. He had no curiosity. It was his chief defect.

DORIAN: What would you say, Harry, if I told you that I had murdered Basil?

LORD HENRY: I would say, my dear fellow, that you were posing for a character that doesn't suit you. All crime is vulgar, just as all vulgarity is crime. It is not in you, Dorian, to commit a murder. I am sorry if I hurt your vanity by saying so, but I assure you it's true. Crime belongs exclusively to the lower orders. I don't blame them in the smallest degree. I should fancy that crime was to them what art is to us, simply a method of procuring extraordinary sensations.

DORIAN: A method of procuring sensations? Do you think, then, that a man who has once committed a murder could possibly do the same crime again? Don't tell me that.

LORD HENRY: Oh! Anything becomes a pleasure if one does it too often. That is one of the most important secrets of life. I should fancy, however, that murder is always a mistake. One should never do anything that one cannot talk about after dinner. But let us pass from poor Basil. I wish I could believe that he had come to such a really romantic end as you suggest; but I can't. I dare say he fell into the Seine off an omnibus, and that the conductor hushed up the scandal. Yes: I should fancy that was his end. I see him lying now on his back under those dull-green waters with the heavy barges floating over him, and long weeds catching in his hair. Do you know, I don't think he would have done much more good work. During the last ten years his painting has gone off very much.

DORIAN: Don't, Harry. The soul is a terrible reality. It can be bought, and sold, and bartered away. It can be poisoned, or made perfect. There is a soul in each one of us. I know it.

LORD HENRY: Do you feel quite sure of that, Dorian?

DORIAN: Quite sure.

LORD HENRY: How grave you are! Don't be so serious. What have you or I to do with the superstitions of our age? No: we have given up our belief in the soul. Tell me, if you can, how you have kept your youth. You must have some secret. I am only ten years older than you are, and I am wrinkled and worn, and yellow and quite awful looking. You are really wonderful, Dorian. You have never looked better than you do tonight. You remind me of the day I first saw you. You were rather cheeky, very shy, and absolutely extra-ordinary. You have changed, of course, but not in appearance. I wish you would tell me your secret. To get back my youth I would do anything in the world; except take exercise, get up early, or be respectable. Youth! There is nothing like it. It's absurd to talk of the ignorance of youth. The only people to whose opinions I listen now with any respect are people much younger than myself. They seem in front of me. Life has revealed to them her latest wonder. As for the aged, I always contradict the aged. I do it on principle. If you ask them their opinion on something that happened yesterday, they solemnly give you the opinions current in 1820, when people wore high stocks . . . believed in everything, and knew absolutely nothing. You are still the same.

DORIAN: I am not the same, Harry.

LORD HENRY: Yes, you are the same.

DORIAN: I *am* a little changed already.

LORD HENRY: You cannot change to me, Dorian. You and I will always be friends.

DORIAN: Yet you poisoned me with a book once. I should not forgive that. Harry, promise me that you will never lend that book to anyone. It does harm.

LORD HENRY: My dear boy, you really are beginning to moralize. You will soon be going about like the converted, the revivalist, warning people against all the sins of which you have grown tired. You are much too delightful to do that. Besides, it is no use. You and I are what we are, and will be what we will be. As for being poisoned by a book, there is no such thing as that. Art has no influence upon action. It annihilates the desire to act. It is superbly sterile. The books that the world calls immoral are books that show the world its own shame. That is all. But we won't discuss literature. Come round tomorrow. I am going to ride at eleven.

DORIAN: Must I really come, Harry?

LORD HENRY: Certainly. The Park is quite lovely now. I don't think there have been such lilacs since the year I met you.

DORIAN: Very well. I shall be here at eleven. Good-night, Harry.

(*As* LORD HENRY *reaches the door he hesitates for a moment, as if he had something more to say. He goes out.*)

FADE

SCENE VI

DORIAN's *rooms. The room is covered in a strange series of lights that throw up all the myriad objects in the room. Almost the nineteenth-century version of a strobe pop scene. Music plays from all quarters, including the streets outside. There are shouts, screams, moans.* DORIAN *comes in, more immaculate than at any time during the action. The rest of the scene is taken up with his examining all the objects in the room in detail, as if he were retracing all the objects and events of his life. People he has known;* SIBYL, HARRY, BASIL *and so on.*

After some time of this, he takes the lamp from the table and goes up to the room where the portrait lies. He unlocks it carefully, goes in and closes the door behind him. Presently, there is a crash, the door opens and DORIAN *is seen stabbing the picture with a knife. It rolls, frame and all, in fragments down on to the stage. The light gutters out and there is a horrifying scream. In the darkness,* FRANCIS *comes in. There is a furious banging at the door and lights flash from outside.* TWO CONSTABLES *enter.*

CONSTABLE: Whose house is this then?

FRANCIS: Mr. Dorian Gray's, sir.

CONSTABLE: Dorian Gray.

(*They push past the servant and flash their lamps into the room. After a while, they pick out the remains of the portrait. Then the beam flashes very brightly on to the body of a shrivelled crone in evening dress, draped over the stairs, a knife and canvas still in his hands. It is the old carcass of* DORIAN GRAY.)

CURTAIN